Order Without Design

Information Production and Policy Making

Order Without Design

Information Production and Policy Making

MARTHA S. FELDMAN

STANFORD UNIVERSITY PRESS   1989
STANFORD, CALIFORNIA

Stanford University Press, Stanford, California
© 1989 by the Board of Trustees of the Leland
Stanford Junior University
Printed in the United States of America
CIP data appear at the end of the book

Published with the assistance of a special grant from
the Stanford University Faculty Publication Fund to
help support nonfaculty work originating at
Stanford.

For my parents

Preface

I SPENT one and one-half years—from May 1980 to December 1981—observing and participating in the work of the policy office of the U.S. Department of Energy. During that time I gathered data both formally and informally. These data provide the basis for this book. The understanding of the role of bureaucratic analysts expressed in this book has grown out of my attempts to make sense of what I observed and experienced during this period.

I have developed a notion about the role of interpretation in policy making. I have focused on the process of information production so that I could build ideas about the policy process based on my observations of behavior. I hope, however, that this focus does not convey the impression that the process of information production is more important than the process of interpretation. Indeed, information production is only one facet of the interpretation process. It is, however, a facet that can be observed and from which one can begin to understand the larger process to which it contributes.

In developing the ideas expressed in this book I was influenced by many observers of organizations and political processes. Most of these intellectual debts are acknowledged in the book. However, the influence of some scholars on my work is more subtle than can be expressed in citations. There are three areas where this is particularly true. One of these is in understanding the interactions between organizations and political processes. Here I have gone repeatedly to the works of Herbert Kaufman and Charles E. Lindblom. Another area concerns the role of perception in political processes. I have learned a great deal about this topic from the writings of Murray Edelman and from both the works of and my work with W. Lance Bennett. The third area concerns the role of information and ambiguity in decision processes. Reading the works of and having an opportunity to work with James G. March has developed my understandings in this area.

The ideas of these scholars expressed in their writings, in their comments on my work, and in conversation have helped me to develop the understanding of the role of bureaucratic information in policy making expressed in this book. Their scholarly endeavors have provided a background of insights that have made my work richer. I am very grateful to them.

I am indebted to many others as well for helping me write this book. I must, first of all, thank the people in the policy office of the U.S. Department of Energy during the period of my research for providing the data for this report. I am particularly grateful to the staff members who participated in structured data gathering. Without their considerable efforts much of the data used in this report would not exist. I am also thankful to the many people I came in contact with through my position as a policy analyst who took an interest in my research and helped me to see the policy office from different perspectives.

This book started out as a dissertation. It was financially supported by the A. W. Mellon Foundation, the Brookings Institution, the Hoover Institution, the National Institute for Mental Health Organization Research Training Program at Stanford University, and the Spencer Foundation.

I am grateful to Kennette Benedict, Gary Brewer, Robert Coulam, Susan Krieger, Lawrence Lynn, Nancy MacRae, Joanne Martin, Daniel Okimoto, Richard Smith, and J. Serge Taylor for reading and commenting on drafts of the dissertation. Many of their thoughtful comments are incorporated in the final version of this book.

I especially thank Michael D. Cohen, Elisabeth Hansot, James March, and Lee S. Sproull for helping me throughout the period of research and writing for the dissertation. Each spent many hours talking with me about the ideas in the dissertation, and all were particularly supportive during a time when I particularly needed it.

Many people have helped me to revise the dissertation into a book. Bob Axelrod, Severin Borenstein, Tom Hammond, Edie Goldenberg, Bengt Jacobsson, Peter Manning, Kim Scheppele, Bruce Spencer, and John Van Maanen provided comments and encouragement in various stages of the writing. Michael Cohen and James March have continued to help me think through the issues I deal with in this book. I am particularly grateful to Don Herzog and Janet Weiss, who spent many hours reading various drafts of the manuscript and talking with me over many lunches about what I was saying and what I could say.

I thank Julie Higgs and Anna Rockhill for proofreading and assistance with the bibliography. I thank Judith Brown, Tonia Ferenczy, Judy Jackson, and Linda McMichael for secretarial support. I thank Jonathan Stick for helping with the index. I thank Ellen Smith for being a very helpful and supportive editor.

M.S.F.

Contents

PART I

Introduction

CHAPTER 1

The Paradox of Producing
Information

DURING THE one and one-half years I spent in the policy office of the U.S. Department of Energy,* I was continually struck by the paradox that is explored in this chapter and that led to the ideas explored in the rest of this book. When I explained to the members of this office that I was interested in how the policy office produced information and how it was used, I was met time and again with the response that the information is not used. The analysts told me story after story about papers they had written that had never even been read by the policy makers who were currently concerned with the issues those papers discussed.

Yet, at the same time, I saw these analysts working hard to produce the information they claimed would be ignored. They worked late nights and weekends. They poured energy into deliberations and negotiations with analysts in other offices. They spent hours gathering information and analyzing it. They became angry when their contributions to a report were overlooked by those in charge of producing the report.

The paradox was most succinctly stated by an analyst talking at an office party. He said that when he writes a contract for a paper to be written for the policy office, he knows that the paper will not be used. "It won't be used," he said, "for one of the fol-

---

*Throughout the text I refer to this office as "the policy office" rather than by formal title because the office was reorganized twice during the period of study and, thus, had three different titles. The reorganizations did not substantially change the responsibilities of the policy office, the means of carrying them out, or the personnel who performed the work.

lowing reasons—either it won't get done in time, or it won't be good enough, or the person who wanted it done will have left and no one will know what to do with it, or the issue will no longer exist." He said that the reports are almost never used, yet he thinks that they should be written. They should be written, he said, because the analyses contained in them should be done.

Thus, the analysts believe that the work is important and ought to be performed even though they believe that it is neither appreciated nor even attended to by policy makers. This paradoxical view is not limited to people working in the bureaucracy. Congress, for example, mandates the establishment of policy offices in new departments and yearly asks for numerous reports from these offices. Yet the reports appear to have little impact on the actions taken by the legislature.

There are many possible explanations for this paradox. Information is often commissioned and not used for a variety of practical, organizational, and political reasons (Feldman and March, 1981; Lindblom and Cohen, 1979; Lynn, 1978; Orlans, 1973; Rich, 1981a, 1981b; Rule, 1978; Weiss, 1977, 1978; Wilensky, 1967). In this book I explore a particular explanation that examines the discrepancy between what the analysts want to produce and what is actually produced. Briefly, I claim that the analysts who produce the information would like to produce clear and straightforward analyses or interpretations that could be used to make decisions or solve problems. By contrast, the way that the process works results in a type of information that is much less decisive than that. While the information that analysts produce may not be what they want to produce, it is both important and unique.

A description of what these analysts do helps to clarify this argument. These analysts produce information in the form of written reports (they also sometimes give oral briefings as well). These reports take a variety of forms. For example, they may be interdepartmental reports to the president; they may be testimony before Congress; they may be comments on a proposed regulation. So far, this is pretty straightforward. The manner in which the information is produced is what is not straightforward.

The process of producing information in this setting, in fact, mitigates against the production of clear and concise analyses that are decision-relevant. In this process analysts representing many different interests need to combine their many points of view on the issue they are writing about. The result is seldom a forceful analysis or a strong presentation of a position. Positions and analyses are watered down. Obtaining consensus on the report often means either leaving out so many points that the paper is bland or putting in so many points that it is wishy-washy.

One of the examples of report writing used in Chapter 4 illustrates this process and its outcome. The report involved comments on a proposed regulation by three parts of the Department of Energy: a policy office, a legal office, and a program office that dealt with economic regulation. The regulation was about how the railroads establish that they are making adequate revenues. The Department of Energy interest in the matter pertained to the price of shipping coal. The representatives from the policy office and the legal office did not believe that the regulation would have much effect on the prices railroads charged for shipping coal; the representatives from the program office thought it would create a hardship for coal shippers by giving the railroads an opportunity to increase the price of shipping coal. These two groups argued with one another. Each group did analyses, and each disagreed about the validity of the other's analysis. Each hoped to have the comments reflect their perception of the regulation. As the deadline for submitting the comments approached, the two groups were no closer to agreement. Yet they all knew that if comments were to be submitted, all three offices had to sign them. That meant that all of these representatives had to agree about the content of the comments. At the last minute, they put parts of each position together and submitted comments that represented neither position very well.

This example is an extreme one; positions are not usually so completely polarized. However, it does illustrate how the need for consensus among representatives of many interests influences the type of information that is contained in the resulting papers. This point will be elaborated in the course of this book.

There is some groundwork necessary before proceeding. There are several terms used in this book that are important for understanding the argument, and these are explained below. Following that is a brief discussion of the work bureaucratic analysts do and its relation to the paradox described at the beginning of the chapter.

Terminology

Bureaucratic Analysts

Throughout this book the analysts discussed are referred to as bureaucratic analysts. They are people who have analytic responsibilities within a bureaucratic structure. Their duties involve interaction with other analysts and require hierarchical approval. They do not generally have managerial responsibilities.*

Though the term policy analyst is more common and refers to some of the same people, it is not used in this book for three reasons. One is that the job title of some of the people discussed was "policy analyst," yet other people with job titles such as "program analyst" or "regulatory analyst" are also discussed. Second, while all of these titles existed in the policy office, not all of the people portrayed in this book worked in policy offices. Some of them worked in program offices, general counsel's offices, and regulatory administrations. Finally, in the literature the term policy analyst often refers to people who are outside the bureaucratic structure. Academics who analyze policies are, for instance, often referred to as policy analysts. The term bureaucratic analyst captures the fact that these are people who practice analytical skills in a bureaucratic context. Both of these aspects of the position are important to understanding the work bureaucratic analysts do.

Uncertainty and Ambiguity

Uncertainty and ambiguity are terms that are central to understanding the purpose of information production and the role of information in organizational decisions and actions. Understanding the difference between the two is important to understanding the role of information that bureaucratic analysts produce. Uncertainty can be resolved by obtaining certain speci-

---

*Bureaucratic analysts are described in further detail in Chapter 2. Also see Meltsner (1976) for a good discussion of types of bureaucratic analysts, and see Weimer and Vining (1988), pp. 9–11, for a discussion of where bureaucratic analysts work.

fiable pieces of information. These pieces of information may be very expensive, or they may not even exist. For example, what the weather will be like tomorrow is uncertain and can only be resolved by gaining information that does not exist today. However, when the information is available, the uncertainty can be resolved.

Because the information needed to resolve uncertainty is often either very expensive or impossible to obtain, we have developed methods of analysis that allow us to make good guesses about what that information might be. So, for example, we have methods of analyzing data relevant to the weather that allow us to make a good guess about what tomorrow will be like. This information helps us to make decisions about the appropriate activities, clothing, and so forth.

Some public policy questions that illustrate uncertainty might include the following: What is the rate of spread of the AIDS virus and how can it be slowed? What will be the effect of an increase or decrease in the defense budget on military troop strength? What will be the cost of providing long-term medical care for the elderly and disabled? Analyses can help us find answers to these questions. Unlike physical phenomena, however, analyses of public policy issues may influence the eventual outcome. This makes it somewhat harder to know whether the analysis provided the "correct" answer or, indeed, to define a correct answer.

Ambiguity, by contrast, cannot be resolved simply by gathering information. Ambiguity is the state of having many ways of thinking about the same circumstances or phenomena. Thus, more information is not directly relevant to resolving ambiguity. For instance, while we can know with certainty what the weather is like, we cannot resolve the question of whether it is good weather or bad through gathering information. That determination, to the extent that we can come to a consensus about it, depends on a process of interpretation. This process includes discussions of what is relevant as well as what value to give the many relevant features of the question. Are you talking about good for growing crops, good for taking a walk, good for writing a book? If all three are important, is writing a book as valuable for the resolution of this ambiguity as growing crops?

Some public policy questions that illustrate ambiguity follow.

Should the prevention of AIDS be dealt with primarily as a health or an education issue? What is the relation between troop strength and national security? What is national security? Is providing long-term medical care for the elderly and disabled an appropriate role for government? Should the government provide medical care for everyone? What are the long-term effects of welfare?

Ambiguity often exists when a commonly held perception of the issue is not well defined. People may come to a consensus about questions of ambiguity, but there are no right or wrong answers. There is often consensus about potentially ambiguous issues within a culture. The people in many countries have, for example, agreed that providing health care is an appropriate activity for the government to engage in. Other countries have no such consensus. Such decisions are generally considered "political" and are determined through political procedures.

Information is not, however, irrelevant to these decisions. Information can be useful in exploring ambiguity. For this purpose it is important to know about the alternative conceptions of the issue, to know what concerns are relevant to each way of perceiving the issue and to understand the points of similarity and discrepancy in the interpretations. In considering whether an AIDS prevention program should be located primarily in the Department of Education or in the Department of Health and Human Services, it would be useful to know how the people in each department conceptualize the problem and what programs they are capable of mounting. It would be useful to know how the approaches of the two organizations are likely to differ. This information, however, will not resolve the question. In the end AIDS will continue to be both a health and an education issue, and people will be able to make powerful arguments on either side.

Any time we confront a complex reality, ambiguity is possible. The ambiguity may be resolved by shared agreements about what is important and what is unimportant. These agreements are reached through a process of interpretation. It is a process that is continuous. New issues arise about which there are no agreements, and old agreements are called into question.

Uncertainty and ambiguity exist side by side in issues of public policy. We may be able to resolve the uncertainty about the effect of decreasing the defense budget on troop strength. However, we need to think about what we mean by national security before we understand the relation between the defense budget and this concept.

Interpretation

Interpretation is a word used often in this book. It is the process of giving meaning. Since ambiguous issues have no clear meaning, they need to be interpreted. Policy issues need to have meaning before they can be acted upon (this is discussed in more detail in Chapter 2). The meaning they acquire helps to determine what actions are appropriate. Lack of clear meaning often results from the fact that there are many possible ways of perceiving the issue; these may be thought of as competing interpretations. Interpretation also takes place when these competing perceptions are taken together to make sense of an issue.

Take, for example, an issue dealt with in the report on energy transportation written by members of the Departments of Energy and Transportation (National Energy Transportation Study, 1980; this report is discussed in detail in Chapter 4). The issue discussed here is the financial condition of the railroads, a critical issue in coal transportation. In this case, each department had a different way of looking at the railroads' financial condition.

The interpretation of the Department of Transportation analysts was optimistic about the railroads. They said that the railroads are generally in good shape to continue being the nation's major coal haulers. They also said that to the extent that the railroads have problems, the coal traffic itself will help keep them strong. This interpretation was consistent with the concern of the Department of Transportation for maintaining and strengthening the viability of the railroads.

The interpretation made by the Department of Energy analysts was consistent with their concern for making coal competitive with other fuels. They said that the railroads are in weak financial condition and are subsidizing other operations through the high prices they charge for coal. They can charge these high prices because there are no reasonable alternate means for shipping coal long inland distances. The high price of transporting coal reduces its ability to replace foreign oil, and at the time reducing dependence on imported oil was the primary goal of the Department of Energy. Therefore, they proposed support for the development of alternate means of transporting coal.

These two interpretations were based on the same data. They were simply different ways of making sense of the same issue. Their differences derive, in part, from what concerns are considered relevant. For the Department of Transportation analysts, the viability of the railroads was a major concern, while for the Department of Energy analysts the cost of coal was primary.

These two interpretations were combined in the final report. It stated that the railroads appear capable of financing both new rolling stock and new rail lines (both of which are necessary for continuing to be able to haul the nation's coal), but that its financial condition is the "weakest of any transportation mode" (p. 64), that "a history of bankruptcies and reorganizations has limited access to capital markets for some of the railroads" (p. 64), and that mergers that have been occurring create additional financial uncertainty. It also said that "national transportation goals such as improving the viability of the railroad industry should be balanced with energy goals such as increasing coal use to reduce oil use" (p. 65). Thus, the report contained parts of each argument about the financial condition of the railroads and a statement about the relation between the goals of the two departments.

This combination of two (or more) points of view is also an interpretation of the issue. It gives meaning to an issue by showing different facets, or "faces," of the issue. Ideally, the connections among the facets are also drawn. The consistency or coherence of such an interpretation depends on the amount of discrepancy among the points of view that make it up.

Thus, both a coherent point of view and combinations of points of view are called interpretations. This creates some confusion, which might be avoided by calling the former a point of view and the latter an interpretation. The problem with this solution is that coherence is relative. The former only appears coherent in relation to the latter. Take the financial condition of the railroads again. Within both the Departments of Energy and Transportation there were disputes among analysts from different offices about how to make sense of the issue. Only in relation to the larger differences between departments did each department's view appear coherent.

Problem Solving and Issue Interpretation

Problem solving and issue interpretation are two processes that affect policy issues (they are described in greater detail in Chapter 2). Issue interpretation is a process of agreeing about how to perceive an issue (who is agreeing can be left open here, since the relevant actors change with the context). Issue interpretations logically precede problem solving. The more consensus there is about the meaning of an issue, the less interpretation is necessary. Agreement about how to view the issue includes agreement about what is problematic about it. If problems are defined, then their solution can be attempted. These attempts constitute the process of problem solving.

This logical sequence is not necessarily the actual sequence. The two processes, in practice, are more intertwined. A proposed solution, for instance, may presuppose an interpretation of the issue. For example, the Department of Energy suggestion to support alternatives to railroad transport of coal is based on the interpretation of the financial condition of the railroads and its effect on coal prices. The proposal could be adopted without agreement on the interpretation.

Though these two processes are intertwined, it is useful to distinguish between them. Problem solving is a process that is relatively clearly defined. It assumes the specification of a problem. How to build a bridge across a particular body of water or how to inoculate large populations against a virus are examples of problems to be solved. Though the problem may be very difficult or even impossible to solve, the quest is clearly defined. The process is similar and related to the process of resolving uncertainty.

By contrast, the process of issue interpretation has few constraints and no known end. Issues such as space flight, health care, and energy are continually being interpreted and reinterpreted. New concerns are associated with them; old concerns become irrelevant. The process of exploring ambiguity is intrinsic to the process of issue interpretation.

The Work of Bureaucratic Analysts

Bureaucratic analysts engage in both problem solving and issue interpretation. Some of the work bureaucratic analysts do is used directly in policy making. Examples of this are rare, but it does happen (see Chapter 8 for an example that took place in the course of this study). Some of what analysts do also helps to legitimate policies that are made. The following example illustrates both influencing and legitimating policies. Analysts from the policy office and a program office, aided by a group of consultants, looked at the problem of gasoline prices. They analyzed several alternatives under different conditions, and they kept coming to the conclusion that the prices should be decontrolled. This conclusion was contrary to current policy. Their superiors suggested new alternatives and new conditions, but the conclusion was still the same. Finally, after more than a year and slightly before the Reagan administration took office, their superiors were convinced. Decontrol was suggested in a speech by the head of the regulatory office. As the analyst said, it "proved that you could teach people . . . and it helped the Reagan administration, since the staff had already changed [the hierarchical superiors'] minds" (interview 28).

Most often, however, the work that bureaucratic analysts do is neither so narrowly focused nor so decision-relevant. This is, in part, a result of the way information is produced in this setting. This process results in information that provides a variety of perspectives rather than a single focused interpretation or analysis. Though analysts may intend to produce such a focused report, there is seldom sufficient consensus for them to do so.

This process leads to a great deal of frustration on the part of bureaucratic analysts. They often start out a paper-writing assignment with a fairly firmly held notion of what concerns are relevant to the issue and what would be the appropriate actions for decision makers to take. They have gathered information and done analyses that have convinced them and, they think, should convince others. Then, in the process of coordinating with other units or departments, some concerns they consider relevant are contested, and other concerns they consider irrelevant are promoted. The actions they think decision makers should take are disputed. The analyses they have done are modified or become irrelevant. The end product is not the clarifying, decision-relevant report they wanted to produce, but a jumble of information from many different perspectives.

This raises one of the fascinating features of the paradox this chapter began with. Bureaucratic analysts engage in behaviors that produce a result they do not like. Their belief in the importance of clarity and problem solving influences their attitude about their work, but it appears to have only a limited influence on what they produce. Instead, constraints that exist in the context in which they work shape the patterns of their behavior and the results of their labor.

Beliefs and Behavior

The effects of beliefs on behavior are limited by environmental constraints. As Erving Goffman has said, "defining situations as real certainly has consequences, but these may contribute very marginally to the events in progress; in some cases only a slight embarrassment flits across the scene in mild concern for those who tried to define the situation wrongly. All the world is not a stage—certainly the theater isn't entirely. (Whether you organize a theater or an aircraft factory, you need to find places for cars to park and coats to be checked, and these had better be real places, which, incidentally, had better carry real insurance against theft)" (Goffman, 1974, p. 1).

Just as real people and cars may make demands on the theater, features of the policy-making context make demands on the way information is produced for making policy. The demands are met with organizational routines. In the case of theaters these include procedures for dealing with coat checking and insurance policies. In the case of policy making, one place these routines can be found is in the procedures for producing information.

Constraints on Producing Information

At least two features of policy making create demands on information production. One is the inability of policy makers (or anyone else) to know what problems they need information about. The other is the desire of policy makers to have information from many sources.

Policy makers are unable to specify their future needs for information for several reasons (Kingdon, 1984; Lynn, 1978; Weiss, 1980). Sometimes problems appear suddenly as a result of unpredictable events. Natural catastrophes, epidemics, or military maneuvers by foreign countries can create sudden needs for information. The process is generally more banal than this, however, and there is no clear explanation of why many policy issues emerge at the time they do (Kingdon, 1984). The process is influenced by changes in systematic indicators, by regularly scheduled organizational processes such as budget cycles, oversight reviews, and program renewals, by the attention of politically relevant audiences and actors, and by the absence of other, more pressing issues.

This inability to predict future information needs creates problems for people and organizations charged with providing information. These problems are exacerbated by the desire of policy makers to have information that reflects many interests. Good information takes time to produce; anyone who has engaged in research recognizes that fact. Policy makers, however, want more than just good information. They want information that has been agreed upon by people and organizations representing many different and often conflicting interests.

These two features of the context of policy making constrain the process of information production. They place certain demands on the process that would not be there if the need for information were more predictable and required less coordination. The demands on the process have been met by organizational routines. Three of the routines in information production are the concurrence process, the paper-writing routine, and the organization of expertise. These routines and their effects on the production of information are examined throughout this book.

Why Do Bureaucratic Analysts Persist?

Though bureaucratic analysts engage in the routines discussed above, they do not much like the information that is produced as a result. They frequently complain about the end result, but they continue to do analyses, to propose solutions to the problems that they perceive, and to promote the positions supported by their organizations. Why? There are many answers to this question. The first is that it is their job to promote the positions their organizations have taken in the past or positions that are consistent with the interests their organization represents. While the expectations of superiors may be sufficient motivation, there are other reasons for bureaucratic analysts to do their jobs well. They are, of course, dependent on their jobs for salary and other material benefits. Though they work in the civil service, promotions and even maintaining one's job are not completely assured. They are also motivated by the demands and expectations of their peers. By working hard, one can gain a good reputation with peers as well as with hierarchical superiors. Having a good reputation among people you work with also enhances career opportunities both in and outside the bureaucracy.

Another reason that bureaucratic analysts work hard at doing analyses and promoting positions or solutions to problems is that they value the work. This is what they have learned to do in their university training, and it is what they know how to do well. Being involved in problem solving is important and even glamorous. Though the analysts' work is seldom used directly in decision making, it is very noticeable and memorable when it does happen. For many, the possibility of such a contribution to policy making is worth the frequent experience of frustration.

Finally, bureaucratic analysts do what they do because it is the only way that they can hope to have an influence on policy making. They cannot do anything about the process that forces them to combine their positions with those of analysts from other organizations. Therefore, the only way they can have any influence on how decision makers perceive an issue is to give their best effort to have the paper reflect as much of their positions and analyses as possible. As a result, rather than giving up, they may put even more effort into developing the information and analyses to promote their positions.

About This Book

Thus, the answer to the paradox of producing information has many facets. Policy makers do not use the analysts' papers to make decisions in part because the kind of papers they produce are not generally useful for decision making. There are also other practical, organizational, and political reasons for not using these papers. Yet analysts continue to work hard at producing these papers because it is their job, they value the work, it is their major means of influencing policy making, and they cannot do anything about the constraints on the process that make their papers less relevant for problem solving.

The existence of this paradox suggested to me that there was something worth investigating in the relation between analysts and the work they produce. The "answer" to the paradox is, in many ways, less important than the exploration. In the process of coming to understand the conditions that create the paradox, I explored many features of the work bureaucratic analysts do, of the way organizational constraints and the structure of their work influence what they do, and of the possible effects their work may have. These topics, briefly outlined in this chapter, are discussed in greater depth in the remaining chapters.

This book is organized in parts. Part I is the introduction. Following the overview given in this opening chapter, Chapter 2 discusses theories of decision making and their applicability to policy making. In Chapter 3 the methodological underpinnings of this study, the methods of data gathering, and the context of the study are explained.

Part II presents in detail what bureaucratic analysts do when they produce information. Chapter 4 gives examples of report writing. Chapter 5 discusses what bureaucratic analysts do when they take care of an issue. Chapter 6 explores some of the complications of the role played by bureaucratic analysts as they perform the tasks described in Chapters 4 and 5. The data presented in this section (and in Appendixes A and B) are used as examples throughout the book.

In Part III the contribution that bureaucratic analysts make to policy making is examined. Chapter 7 deals with the reasons that the behavior cannot conform to expectations established by a rational or bounded rational notion of decision making (see Chapter 2 for an explanation of these terms). It explores the relationship between a context that does not encourage rational or boundedly rational action and the need for inventories of interpretations. Chapter 8 develops the notion that bureaucratic analysts produce interpretations of issues and that they produce a unique kind of interpretation. It also deals with the question of the use of these interpretations in policy making. Chapter 9 discusses the discrepancy between the bureaucratic analysts' perspective and the interpretive perspective.

Part IV explores the implications of this study. Chapters 10 and 11 deal with the implications of the interpretive perspective for the role of bureaucratic analysts and the organizing of bureaucratic analysts, respectively. Chapter 12 concludes the book with a discussion of the process of information production in organizations.

CHAPTER 2

Interpretation in Decision Making and Policy Making

THIS STUDY is based on both empirical observation and theoretical understandings. Though making the observations is substantially independent of theory, making sense of the observations is heavily dependent on theory. Theories of organizational decision making and information use inform the interpretation of behavior in this study.

Models of Decision Making

Means-end rationality is one way of making sense out of human behavior (Hume, 1980; Weber, 1978). The extension of this notion to decision making is a theory of rational choice. This form of decision making involves the following steps. First, decision makers recognize the existence of a problem. Then they specify the goals and preferences that define an optimal solution. They consider all alternative solutions. They use information to choose the solution among these alternatives that maximizes the likelihood of achieving the goals and preferences (see Allison, 1971; Downs, 1957; Gramlich, 1981; Lindblom, 1959; Luce and Raiffa, 1957; and M. Taylor, 1975, for descriptions of this model).

A modification of this model called bounded rationality resulted from the observation that because of cognitive limits to human attention and organizational limits to the amount of available information, it is often impossible to consider all possible alternative solutions. As a result, Herbert Simon (1956) suggested that people "satisfice" rather than maximize—rather than looking for the absolute best solution, they look for one that meets some acceptable standards. The notion of bounded rationality broadens the original model and makes it more realistic by acknowledging uncertainty. However, it retains the basic notion that the process of decision making begins with establishing what the problem is and what the goals or priorities (e.g., cost, speed) are for solving it.

Examples of such decision making usually occur around large decisions that are seen as isolated events. For instance, the decision to make a major purchase or an organization's decision to build a new building or start a new program may be rational in the sense that goals and priorities are established and action taken in accordance with them (this is, of course, only one sense of the word rational, but it is the one used throughout this book). Crises are also instances in which such rational action may occur.

While in the abstract the model is a perfectly sensible way to make decisions, many scholars have shown that the conditions necessary for this sequence of steps are often unattainable (Elster, 1983; March and Simon, 1958; Nelson and Winter, 1982). In particular, students of politics, psychology, and organizations have discussed at length the obstacles to this form of decision making (Cyert and March, 1963; Kahneman, Slovic, and Tversky, 1982; Kaufman, 1977; Lindblom, 1959, 1968; March and Simon, 1978; Nisbett and Ross, 1980; Steinbruner, 1974; Wildavsky, 1979; Wilensky, 1967).

One problem identified by students of decision making is that behavior is not always guided by a set of well-defined goals and preferences. People and organizations often have multiple and conflicting goals (Cyert and March, 1963). As a result, decision processes are sometimes ways of taking action while avoiding direct conflict among goals. Models based on this notion describe decision making in terms of routines or standard procedures. Thus, behavior is described as a continuous sequence of steps (Cyert and March, 1963), as part of a feedback loop (Steinbruner, 1974), and as incremental adaptation (Lindblom, 1959). In this form of decision making, the problems are still specifiable, but goals are not agreed upon.

Hiring practices and budgeting procedures are routines for

making very difficult decisions without always specifying goals (Wildavsky, 1984). In hiring decisions, people may not be able to agree on a description of the person that they would like to hire, though they may agree that a particular person is appropriate (the opposite may also occur). In this case, the procedure used for hiring allows the organizational members to move past the conflict and to take some action. They look at applications. They interview people. They hire someone. Lindblom has suggested that the same phenomenon occurs in legislatures where at times conservatives and liberals support the same legislation for different reasons (Lindblom, 1959). If they had to agree on the goal of the legislation first, they would not arrive at the same conclusion.

Problem solving can also be seen as part of a larger organizational process (Cohen and March, 1974; Cohen, March, and Olsen, 1972; Weick, 1979). The process that ends in a decision or action does not always begin with a clearly defined problem. This observation brings the whole sequence of rational decision making into doubt. If it is not clear what the problem is, then it is difficult to specify goals for resolving it or to generate alternative solutions. Thus, as this feature of rationality has been questioned, the whole notion of decision making has been broadened. One version of these models is called the "garbage can model," or decision making under ambiguity. It illustrates that the standard decision-making resolution of a solution being matched to a problem is just one of many possibilities as streams of problems and solutions meet streams of participants and opportunities to make choices (Cohen, March, and Olsen, 1972; March and Olsen, 1976).

An example of such decision making occurs when solutions precede problems. This may be the result of technological development. The ability to put astronauts into space occurred before we had developed ideas about why it was important or what problems it would solve (Atkinson and Shafritz, 1985). Similarly, our understanding of the need for computers in organizations developed after they became widely available.

This new perspective on decision making reverses the traditional relationship between the interpretive efforts made by organizational members and problem solving. Traditionally, efforts to understand the environment, the organization, and the relationship between individual action, organizational action, and environmental responses have been valued by participants and scholars as they relate to the pursuit of goals (Scott, 1981). The new perspective suggests that because the world requires interpretation in order to be understood, these efforts are not relevant *only* as they enhance the pursuit of goals but are important *regardless* of their relation to action. Even though rationality and, therefore, problem solving are what is valued, the world is such that we must interpret, whether or not the consequent understanding results in action.

Decision Making Under Ambiguity

There are two slightly divergent versions of this conception. They have been presented by March and a variety of coauthors (Cohen and March, 1974; Cohen, March, and Olsen, 1972; Feldman and March, 1981; March, 1978; March and Olsen, 1976; March and Sevon, 1984; hereafter, I will use the term "March et al." to designate these authors) and by Weick (1979).

March et al. claim to "remain in the tradition of viewing organizational participants as problem solvers and decision makers" (March and Olsen, 1976, p. 21). However, they propose a way of viewing organizations that gives primary importance to the question of "how . . . individuals and organizations make sense of their experience and modify behavior in terms of their interpretations of events" (March and Olsen, 1976, p. 56). Weick leans in the opposite direction and, at times, seems to deny any importance to problem solving. He presents organizations as means of managing equivocality. He says that "we are concerned with ways in which organizations make sense out of the world and of the fact that they spend the majority of their time superimposing a variety of meanings on the world" (Weick, 1979, p. 175).

Though there are differences between the two perspectives presented by these two groups, the fundamentals are quite similar. Both claim that in many, if not most, situations organizational members engage in interpreting events and contexts. This interpretive process is necessary for organizational members to understand and to share understandings about such features of the organization as what it is about, what it does well and poorly, what the problems it faces are, and how it should resolve them. For both groups the characterization of many of the events and contexts that the organization deals with are crucial to their perspective. They both use similar concepts for this purpose. March et al. use the concept of ambiguity. Weick uses equivocality. Ambiguity as used by March et al. implies a lack of clarity in the meaning; no one meaning is given, and there may be many meanings. Equivocality implies that more than one meaning is given.

Whether the situation has many meanings or no clear meaning, the issue for the organization is to make sense out of it. As Weick says, "it is the richness and multiplicity of meanings that can be superimposed on a situation that organizations must manage" (1979, p. 174). March and Olsen express a similar sentiment from a more individual perspective: "Individuals try to make sense out of their experience, even when that experience is ambiguous or misleading and even when that learning does not lead to organizational actions. They impose order, attribute meaning, and provide explanations" (1976, p. 67). In either case the issue for the organization is making sense out of the ambiguous or equivocal phenomena.

Choice and organizational action are sometimes an outcome of this sense-making behavior.* Often, however, sense making does not result in action. It may result in an understanding that action should not be taken or that a better understanding of the event or situation is needed. It may simply result in members of the organization having more and different information about the ambiguous issue. Problem solving may be what we value about what organizations do, but it is not necessarily a very complete description of what they do. This suggests that the traditional notion that problem solving is the primary function of an organization is a statement about values more than one of empirical observation (Feldman and March, 1981).

The Role of Information in Decision Making

The role of information changes according to which kind of decision making is taking place. In the rational and bounded rational models, information provides the means of choosing the

---

*Of course, organizational action may also arise from standard operating procedures or other sources that do not involve conscious sense making.

optimal or satisfactory solution. The information needed is a function of the specified goals. For example, if keeping costs down is a primary goal, then cost comparisons of alternatives will be important information.

In the incremental models information is important feedback that motivates actions as well as being useful in looking for solutions. According to these models, the type of information gathered tends to be guided by the focus of the procedure with which it is associated. The search for solutions, for instance, tends to be in the area where other solutions have been found (Cyert and March, 1963). Thus, in hiring processes, organizations often look for new employees where they have found satisfactory employees in the past.

Information has many roles in the garbage can model. It is useful in exploring problems and solutions, in discovering preferences (March, 1978), in maintaining lines of communication (March and Sevon, 1984), and in establishing the legitimacy of decision processes (Feldman and March, 1981). Another role for information implied by the garbage can model is what can be called issue interpretation. According to this model, problems and solutions are not well specified when they enter the decision process. If this is true, then the decision process must include or depend upon a *prior* process whereby problems and solutions become defined (Riker, 1986; Smith, 1984). This process is issue interpretation.

Issue Interpretation in Policy Making

In thinking about issue interpretation, it is useful to begin by imagining the decision process as a linear sequence. The sequence begins when an issue appears. The issue bounces around. People think and write about it. Money is appropriated to study it and perhaps to work on it. As people think about the issue, it becomes associated with certain concerns. As the issue becomes associated with a set of concerns, it comes to be seen as a problem or a solution.

Any topic relevant to policy decisions is an issue. At different points in history the issue may be nonexistent, controversial, or uncontroversial. Space flight is a good example. At some point it was not even possible. Then for a while it was quite controversial. More recently it has become an accepted part of military and technological policies, though the funding for or the purpose of the space flight may still be the subject of conflict.

Space flight has become associated with keeping up with or catching up to the Soviet Union, with national pride, with military might, with technological superiority. These associations were not always obvious. Space flight became associated with many of these concerns after the Soviet launch of Sputnik in 1957. Prior to that launch the Eisenhower administration's policy on space flight had required strict separation of scientific and military purposes. According to scholars in the area, Eisenhower "gave little thought to any relationship between a scientific space program and its bearing on national prestige, national pride, and international politics" (Atkinson and Shafritz, 1985, p. 19). Even after the Sputnik launch, associating space flight with these concerns was not a foregone conclusion. The executive branch under Eisenhower continued for some time to downplay the relationship. Once the association was made, however, space flight became the solution to the problems of national integrity and military security posed by the Sputnik flight.

Once an issue such as this is clearly defined as a problem or a solution, what we normally think of as decision making or policy making can occur. Rational analysis takes place at this point. Interpretation allows boundaries to be established within which analyses can occur. These boundaries help to determine what is relevant and irrelevant to an understanding of the issue. They help to define problems and goals for the resolution of problems. For instance, once space flight became associated with proving military and technical superiority over the Soviet Union, the goals of speed and an undisputable display of superiority became clear. Having people land on the moon fulfilled the need for an undisputable display. The problem that remained was how to do this quickly. Other definitions of the space flight issue might have resulted in different goals.

Once the problems and goals are established, problems can be matched with solutions. Solutions can be funded and implemented. Finally, problems may be solved.

This, of course, is an idealized version of the process. What really happens does not progress in this straightforward manner. For one thing, at any point the process may stop. Issues may appear and never be clearly defined. Analyses are performed before there is consensus on the interpretation of the issue (Sugden and Williams, 1978; Weimer and Vining, 1988). Issues may enter the decision process as problems or solutions but not be matched with corresponding solutions or problems (Cohen, March, and Olsen, 1972). Problems and solutions may be matched, but the solutions never funded or implemented. Solutions that are funded and implemented may not solve the problems they were intended for (Derthick, 1972; Pressman and Wildavsky, 1973; Weatherley and Lipsky, 1977).

The process, furthermore, is not strictly linear. The space flight example illustrates that an issue may change definition as it is matched to a specific problem. Similarly, issues may be defined and redefined even as they are implemented (Baier, March, and Saetren 1986; Brunsson, 1985).

The context of policy making is consistent with decision making under ambiguity. Policy issues seldom take the form of well-defined problems. When they do, it is generally after years of interpretation.

The Role of Bureaucratic Analysts in Issue Interpretation

Issue interpretation is influenced by information from many sources. Events such as the Sputnik launch, public opinion, political leaders' ideologies, Supreme Court decisions, and academic research all influence the way in which public policy issues are perceived (Atkinson and Shafritz, 1985; Derthick and Quirk, 1985; Fritschler, 1983; Muir, 1973; Rein, 1976). The information produced by bureaucratic analysts in public bureaucracies plays a role in this process. It is not generally a spectacular role, but it may be important.

The interpretations produced by bureaucratic analysts are unique. They not only reflect information from many different sources, but also reflect many different interests. When bureaucratic analysts write papers, they choose what facts and concerns to consider relevant to the issue they are writing about. They make this choice under two constraints. One is that the resulting interpretation be consistent with the interests they are representing. The second is that the interpretation be agreed upon by all the offices on the concurrence list for that paper.

Bureaucratic analysts are constrained by the perspective of the interests they represent. Thus, if the issue is energy development, an office concerned with the environment has very different interests from one concerned with economic regulation or one concerned with legal questions. Departments and offices within departments represent different interests and become attached to different ways to think about issues. The department and office that an analyst works for dictate some of the facts and concerns that will be included in writing a paper.

The second constraint on what is included in an interpretation is the concurrence process. Most papers have to be approved by more than one office. This means that more than one perspective or set of interests is represented in the paper. A single interpretation is the result of negotiations among the analysts representing the interests. The negotiation sometimes results in a very bland document. However, it can also produce valuable information about the differences among the perspectives of the organizations involved.

This process provides policy makers with unique information about the ability or inability of various interests to agree on a way of thinking about an issue and its consequences for policy. No other process systematically forces so many diverse interests to confront one another and come to agreement on a way of presenting an issue. The interests that are represented in a paper are determined by both what interests are represented by offices in the bureaucracy and what offices are on the concurrence list for that particular paper.

Issue Interpretation as a Social Process

The process of issue interpretation described in this book, however, does more than simply provide useful information to decision makers. It also encourages a dissemination of informa-

tion to a variety of people for whom the information is relevant.*
The social nature of the process is essential to this result.

Interpretation can be either an individual or a social process.
When policy analysts work for a client, they often have to define
or frame a problem before they proceed to considering solutions
(see Sugden and Williams, 1978 and Weimer and Vining, 1988 for
discussions of how policy analysts can deal with poorly specified or unspecified problems). This is a critical and difficult step
in policy analysis (Weimer and Vining, 1988, pp. 181–94). It is
also an essential precursor to the process of problem solving or
solution analysis. The tasks involved are "very important because they largely determine which goals and methods should
be used to judge the desirability of alternative solutions. This in
turn tends to drive the selection of policy alternatives" (p. 183).
In this individual process, analysts assess their client's situation
and needs, gather information, and consider alternatives. Then
they propose interpretations of issues that form the basis for the
rest of the analysis.

The social process described in this book may begin in the
above manner. Then, however, the analysts confront other analysts who see the issue quite differently. They exchange points
of view and the information their perspectives are based on.
They argue. They try to come to some agreement about what
they can all consent to include in a written report. They each
then try to convince their hierarchical superiors that the perspectives contained in the report are appropriate and that they
should sign off on the report. (Of course, the process does not
always occur just this way, but this is an adequate summary.) In
the course of this process, information has been widely dispersed among the analysts and their hierarchical superiors.
Everyone involved in the process comes away with a changed
understanding of the issue and modified knowledge of the information relevant to the issue. This exchange of information
does not mean that people will agree. It only means that they
will know more about the perceptions of the issue.

The social process of interpretation also frames the issue by

*In this way it resembles the price system as described by Hayek; see Chapter
12 for a more complete discussion of this comparison.

associating it with relevant concerns. Sometimes this frame will be narrow enough to provide the basis for a rational analysis. Often, however, the information dissemination will be the main outcome of the process.

Conclusion

Though this study is based on empirical observation, the theoretical background is also important. Theories serve a number of purposes. In general, theories help us to understand the conditions that produce the observed behavior and to recognize other situations in which similar behavior may occur. In this instance, one can generalize to organizations that deal with issues of ambiguity where members of the organization need to understand the issues.

Theories also help in making choices about which features of the context are most relevant to understanding behavior. Thus, in this case theories of decision making direct attention to the relation between information production, problem solving, and issue interpretation. The observed behavior could be given other meanings if, for instance, theories of group dynamics or social psychology were used to understand it.

The specific theories in this case also help to illuminate the discrepancy between the contribution to policy making that bureaucratic analysts would like to make and the way that much of their work actually contributes to this policy making. The bureaucratic analysts have a rational perspective that assumes either that they are given specified policy problems or that part of their job is to specify the policy problems. The interpretation made here is that much of their work is relevant to but somewhat removed from defining the problem. Rather than specifying problems themselves, they contribute to a process that may result in the specification of policy problems.

The connections between observations and theory are suggested here. Their development requires a more substantial account of the observations, which is provided in Part II. Then, in Part III, the connections between the two are more fully developed.

CHAPTER 3

Method and Data

THIS IS A STUDY of information production and use in the U.S. federal bureaucracy. It is primarily an ethnographic study. I gathered data by being a participant in and observer of the production of information in the executive branch of the U.S. government. Much of the data that is central to this study is behavioral. The interpretation of the data is, however, heavily dependent on an understanding of the context in which the behavior occurred and of the meaning of the behavior for the participants.

This study focuses on the process of information production. It is not the study of an organization but of the behaviors engaged in by people holding a certain type of position within the federal bureaucracy.* The study is, however, organizational, in that it is concerned with how the organizational context and the way work is organized influence the process of information production.

This study is also influenced by the particular organization in which I was located. It reflects the position I held—an analyst in the policy office of the U.S. Department of Energy—and what I was able to see from that position. Though I came into contact with, observed, and worked with analysts from other departments and agencies and from other parts of the Department of Energy, I had more access to interactions with bureaucratic analysts in this office. Thus, my field observations are influenced by my location. I also developed more trusting relationships with the analysts in this office because I saw them more often and because they depended on me as a member of their organization.

---

*I suspect that such positions are also found wherever there are large hierarchical organizations, whether public or private, national, state, or local.

For these reasons, when gathering data in a systematic and obtrusive manner, I relied on the analysts in this office.

I chose to be located in the Department of Energy primarily because of the technological nature of the issues the analysts in this office dealt with. Much of the research suggesting that information has a loose or anarchic rather than a tight or orderly relation to decision making has taken place in organizations that deal with "soft" technologies such as education (Cohen and March, 1974; March and Olsen, 1976; Sproull, Weiner, and Wolfe, 1977; Weiss and Gruber, 1984) or mental health (Weiss and Bucuvalas, 1980). It could be argued that the anarchic nature of decision making in these organizations is simply a result of the technology. If we knew how to teach children or how to make people mentally healthy, the decision-making process would be much more orderly.

In contrast to organizations dealing with education, health, or welfare, the Department of Energy deals with a technology that is much more easily characterized as "hard." Though there are many things we do not know about energy, we do know how to heat houses, run machines, distribute fuels, make and refine fuels, and so forth. Moreover, the outcome of these processes is measurable. We can tell when we are doing better or worse. This study, then, extends the literature on the loosely coupled relationship between information use and decision making into an area of more measurable technologies.

Characteristics of Bureaucratic Analysts

I have called the people I studied bureaucratic analysts. They are highly paid professionals without subordinates (Stinchcombe, 1974). They do not have managerial responsibilities. They generally have Government Service ratings of 11 to 14. They are "experts in a recognized body of knowledge that they make available to the organization" (Kanter and Stein, 1979, p. 89). Though I avoid the term "policy analyst" for reasons stated in Chapter 1, they do the work of policy analysts in that they "provide information about the consequences of choosing different policies" (Meltsner, 1976, p. 1). They work within a hierarchical structure. The production of much of their work depends on cooperation from and interaction with people working in other hierarchical chains within the same department or in other departments or agencies in the executive branch as a whole.

Bureaucratic analysts are young, highly educated, and predominantly male.* The average age of the sample was 35-1/2 years. The 34 analysts interviewed held 36 bachelor's degrees, 26 master's degrees, and 8 doctoral degrees among them. Most of these were in areas of political science, economics, and engineering, though there were master's degrees in business administration, education administration, and physics and bachelor's degrees in a wide range of fields, including art history, education, languages and linguistics, physical sciences, and psychology. Three-quarters of the analysts were men.

Bureaucratic analysts tend to be ambitious. They generally acknowledged that they were attracted to the work because of its high visibility and potentially high impact. The "two-year rule" reflects their ambitiousness. This rule was that people should plan to spend roughly two years in the office. It was considered difficult to have much impact in less time, but if you stayed much longer, there was serious question about your ambition. Many people stayed longer, but the average number of years the interviewed analysts had held the same position within the policy office was two years.

Data and Data Gathering

I gathered data through several means. The foundation of the research was an extended period of participant observation. In

---

*The demographic data I have about bureaucratic analysts comes from interviews with more than half of the analysts in the policy office of the Department of Energy. The sampling procedure is described later in this chapter. There are two concerns about the representativeness of this sample. One is that the Department of Energy was so young that the analysts might be mostly new hires. Many of the people, however, had worked in predecessor organizations and considered their position to be essentially the same. In fact, the average number of years these people said they had worked for the Department of Energy was slightly longer than the four years that the department had been in operation. The average was 4-1/2 years; the maximum was 26 years. The other concern is about the representativeness of the sample to the population of analysts in the policy office. There were two measures available for both the total population and the sample. One was gender. The population had 31 percent women, the sample had 26 percent. The other was age. The population's average age was 36 years, the average age of the sample was 35.6 years.

May 1980 I became a member of the Office of Coal and Synthetic Fuels under the assistant secretary of Policy and Evaluation. My organizational position was the same as that of the people I was studying. My responsibilities were the areas of coal transportation and coal exports. I continued to occupy that position through December 1981. During this time I observed and made field notes on events and conversations and kept extensive files on all organizational activities to which my position allowed access. Chapter 4 is based primarily on these field observations.

My dual role, as participant and observer, was not a secret. While reasonable questions may be raised about the possibility of my presence affecting the behavior I observed, there are several factors mitigating such effects. Probably most important is that the behavior was not of the sort that any single individual could influence. Secondly, I was a part of the research site for such a long time that it seems unlikely that people could continue systematically to alter their behavior in my presence. Finally, there is evidence that I actually became a true member in the eyes of many other members of the organization and the larger community. For example, people I worked with outside of the policy office and people in the policy office would contact me when they heard about a job opening in a field related to the position I held in DOE.

The field observations were supplemented by data gathered through more intrusive methods. This occurred at two times, the first of which was a twelve-week period from December 1980 to March 1981. During this time all of the staff members of the Office of Coal and Synthetic Fuels agreed to report to me weekly. At the beginning of the twelve weeks, each person chose one topic for which she or he had responsibility. They each gave some background information about the topics they chose. At the end of each succeeding week, they would tell me what had happened and what they had done concerning this topic. These reports are discussed in Chapter 5 and presented in full in Appendix B.

The normalcy of this period of observation may be questioned. I do not claim that it is normal in some absolute sense. By the time I gathered these data I had been a participant observer for eight months. I had been waiting for a "normal" period, and none had yet occurred. Various disturbances, called "odd times" by the members of the policy office, occurred throughout the time I was there. The reasons for these odd times changed about every three or four months. The first odd time I encountered was caused by the change in Secretary of Energy from James Schlesinger to Charles Duncan. After that there was the 1980 presidential campaign during which the Department of Energy was a focus of attention and publicity. Then the election occurred. The result was a lame-duck president in office and an incoming president who had vowed to get rid of the department. Next, as the new administration took office, the department was reorganized again. Finally, "reductions in force" began, and employees in many parts of the department were laid off. Though there were no layoffs in the policy office, there was talk of cutting the policy staff back from 120 to 10.

It is possible that there is no such thing as a normal time (I have encountered this "odd times" phenomenon in other organizations I have studied as well). All times have their peculiarities, and at any time an organization is responding to particular changing features of the internal or external environment. After eight months of observing, however, I was convinced that day-to-day activities change little, regardless of the odd time or the reason for it. Students of bureaucracies have pointed out that this is one of the strengths of these organizations (Heclo, 1977; Kaufman, 1981; Weber, 1946). Persistent turbulence may even encourage the performance of daily tasks (Sutton, 1984). One way of coping with the fact that it is always an odd time is to engage in business as usual. If it is not clear that there is ever a calm or "normal" time, then work must proceed during the odd times.

The second round of structured data gathering took place at the end of the period of participant observation, from September to December 1981. During this time, I interviewed 34 bureaucratic analysts from the policy office of the Department of Energy. Because I wanted a broad view of how people in the office perceived the organization and their work rather than a majority view, I drew a "selective" sample for this interview. I interviewed at least half of the members of each division because there were noticeable differences between divisions in the policy office. I started out with a list of the members of each division. Beginning at the top of the list, which was in alphabetical order, I called people to set up interviews. After one or two interviews in a division, I would determine from the interview information and from my own knowledge of the division whether there were people who seemed likely to hold very different attitudes or perceptions of the work. Sometimes, for instance, there was an in-group and some more peripheral people in a division. Sometimes there was one person who performed quite different tasks than the others. Sometimes there was a person who was simply known to have different opinions. The sampling technique provided access to the many different perceptions held by members of the office.

These interviews served two purposes. They covered a wide range of topics, thus providing systematic data about many aspects of the work and the work place. They were also important in that they provided a means of separating observations that were idiosyncratic to me and the position I held from observations that were more widely supported by the experiences of others. In this sense, the interviews served to test some of the ideas that had emerged in the field observations. The interview schedule is in Appendix C. Direct quotes from interviews are identified by interview number (1–34).

Accounting for Behavior

I attempt to give as full an account as possible of the behavior I observed. In order to do this I present the behavior with as little analysis as possible. In Chapters 4, 5, and 6 and in Appendixes A and B, I show what bureaucratic analysts do as they produce reports and engage in tasks relevant to their responsibilities. In later chapters I analyze these behaviors from a number of different perspectives.

I account for this behavior from both a participant's and an observer's viewpoints. I refer to these as the subjective and the objective interpretations, respectively, following the terminology of Alfred Schutz (1967). The subjective interpretation is a condensation of the way in which the participants understand their behavior. Since every participant has many ways of understanding his or her behavior and there are many participants, this interpretation is necessarily a very simplified version of the participants' understandings. The briefest statement of this subjective interpretation is that they understand their behavior as making a direct contribution to solving policy problems.

The objective interpretation is objective in the sense that it is from the outside, not in the sense that it is absolute or value-neutral. It is the way an observer understands the behavior and the available features of the context. Clearly, there are many such objective interpretations. In this case, the interpretation I have made is that the direct contributions bureaucratic analysts make to policy decisions are only one part of a larger process whereby they make indirect contributions to the way policy issues are understood.

I developed this objective interpretation through careful analysis of the behavior and observations about how it deviated from the participant's understanding of it. Thus, the objective interpretation is always presented in contrast to the subjective one. The subjective interpretation derives from the rational or problem-solving perspective. As discussed in Chapter 2, students of organization and of policy making have shown that this perspective does not and cannot accurately characterize a great deal of decision making or policy making. It may appear, therefore, that I use this perspective as a straw man. My purpose is, however, quite different. The point of a straw man argument is to be able to tear it down and construct a more meaningful argument in its stead. My point is that actual behavior deviates from intended behavior. This is important, because it serves as a pointer to the features of the context that inhibit the actors from having control of their behavior. Thus, the analysis of the deviations from expected behavior leads to insights about the context relevant to a richer understanding of the behavior.

This split between intended and actual behavior implies that there are two kinds of motivations for the behavior (Schutz, 1967). One is the intentional motivation. The actor acts in order to achieve some end(s). In this case, the "in-order-to" motives include influencing policy outcomes, earning a salary, and developing a career. The actor also acts because the context elicits certain behavior and precludes others. It makes some behaviors appropriate and others inappropriate. In this case, the "because" motive includes the demands by policy makers for certain types of reports and the rules, roles, and resources that constrain the patterns of behavior for producing these reports. Thus, bureaucratic analysts write papers *in order to* influence policy making and *because* they have responsibility for the issues about which policy makers have requested information.

Much of this book focuses on the objective interpretations and the "because" motives. This is not to say that the subjective interpretations and the "in-order-to" motives are unimportant. On the contrary, these aspects of the behavior are essential to both producing it and understanding it. They are, however, more commonly understood and therefore need less explication.

Results and Generalization

This study is a detailed exploration of one process. I undertook it in an attempt to understand more about how bureaucratic organizations and the analysts they employ participate in the production of information and decisions. I focused more on *what* was going on than on whether or not it was good or functional. For this reason, the study bears greater resemblance to a cultural ethnography than to a case study in which there is an attempt to explain some condition of the organization (Eckstein, 1975; Geertz, 1973; George, 1982).

Through analysis I have developed an interpretation of the behavior and the context I observed. The behavior is strongly influenced, if not determined, by the context. Context is sufficiently varied and complex to resist successful categorization. Not all features of context are unique, however, and some features of context that are fairly common may be important to the development of organizational processes. With this in mind, I have tried to focus on aspects of the context I observed that seemed most likely to be features of everyday life in organizations rather than peculiar features of the setting and the people I observed. Thus, this study should contribute to a body of knowledge about organizations and about policy making, provided we remember to be sensitive to important contextual differences that characterize other settings.

PART II

What Bureaucratic Analysts Do

CHAPTER 4

Report Writing

WRITING PAPERS—of many kinds—is the way that bureaucratic analysts provide information to policy makers. This chapter describes in detail how one paper was written and gives a brief description of two other paper-writing processes. The details of all three cases are used as examples throughout the book.

The Report-Writing Process

Each time a report is written two or more organizations agree on some words or phrases that they find appropriate and relevant to the topic of the paper.* These agreed-upon words or phrases can be used in the future as approved by all signing organizational parts. As circumstances change, the agreement may have to change also. Therefore, periodically the agreements become outdated.

Requests for reports serve to initiate the updating of an agreement. These requests come from various sources, but most will involve related government entities. They trigger the report-writing response, during which prior agreements may be reviewed, new agreements may be made, and old ones may be abandoned.

The process, in general, displays the following pattern. A request for a report of some sort is initiated. The office responsible for the report generates a document, which is sent to the other

---

*The organization may be a division, an office, a department and so forth. It is not necessary here to distinguish between these parts of organizations. I will simply refer to the organizational entity involved as an organization even though it may be part of a larger organization.

offices on the concurrence list. The comments that come back indicate how far from agreement the original statement is. They may also be a measure of how much time will be spent by the analysts in reaching a new agreement.

The analysts then communicate in some way about some aspect of producing the paper. They may talk on the phone, send documents through the mail, or meet face-to-face. They may talk about the content of the report or the process or the people involved or the way they feel about it. Interactions in the process become less intense as some sort of agreement is reached. They may involve fewer people or people of lower hierarchical status or less time or some combination of these. Interactions may even drop to zero.

It is not quite clear when the process will be completed until it is over.

A Case: The National Energy Transportation Study

The case discussed here illustrates the process described above. It is somewhat more involved than many papers because the report is longer and involves the coordination of many parts of two departments. And, of course, no two cases are alike in their details: each is influenced by the particular circumstances under which the report is written. In this case the number of people involved, the level of disagreement, the past history of interactions, and the pressure from higher officials to come to agreement all influence the working out of the process.

The effects of the various interests that the analysts represent also come into play. The paper is a combined effort of analysts from different offices. Each analyst is responsible for specific substantive and organizational interests related to some aspect of the role of each office. These interests cover a broad range of concerns. Analysts make claims about both substantive and procedural concerns, and both types of claims are valid. In this case, for instance, the concerns include promoting a particular substantive argument, making sure that the expertise produced by the office is properly used, ensuring the consistency of this report with other reports or actions being taken by the organization, and simply producing a report that everyone approves of.

These interests influence the negotiations about what information is included in the report and how it is presented.

Summary

The National Energy Transportation Study (1980) is an example of an interdepartmental effort to produce a report for Congress. There was considerable disagreement about the content of the draft that the Department of Transportation had written and some talk in the Department of Energy about not participating in the report writing. The report had been requested by the president as a joint effort from the Department of Energy and the Department of Transportation (DOE and DOT), and it had been recorded in the reporting systems of each department (systems that keep track of assigned responsibilities and associated deadlines). As a result, the report required some attention, even if only to justify not writing it. People at the Department of Transportation had already devoted their time and their organization's resources to writing the report and wanted to see their work come to fruition. On the Department of Energy side, there were some indications from the Secretary's office that DOE participation in the report was important to the Secretary. The office that had "the lead" on this report wanted to look good to the Secretary by producing the desired report. Gradually, other DOE participants became invested in the report in much the same way the Department of Transportation participants had.

Background

The National Energy Transportation Study (NETS) was initially requested by President Carter in his first National Energy Plan, April 1977. It was to be a joint effort by the Departments of Energy and Transportation. It discusses past, current, and projected future needs for transporting coal, petroleum, natural gas, and nuclear materials.

The Participants

Participants in the process included staff members from both the Department of Transportation and the Department of Energy. The five participants from DOT at the first meeting were from the policy office. They were occasionally joined by members of the Office of the General Counsel and the Federal Railroad Administration.

Responsibility for the report in DOE had been assigned to the Office of Energy Supply Transportation in Resource Applications (RA). Other participants in DOE came from the policy office, the Economic Regulatory Administration, the Energy Information Administration, Environment, the Office of the General Counsel, Nuclear Energy, and the Secretary's office.

One of the DOE participants—the office from the Economic Regulatory Administration—saw itself as having an "axe to grind." Although designated the Economic Regulatory Administration in this discussion, this group was from only one office in that part of DOE and should not be taken as representative of the whole. This group maintained that the railroads were being allowed to make extraordinary profits at the expense of the coal consumer. They felt that other government entities such as the Federal Railroad Administration and the Interstate Commerce Commission were too soft on the railroads. The mission of this office was to correct that bias. Other parts of DOE were not necessarily seen as allies. In fact, this office had a history of conflict over this issue with the Office of Energy Supply Transportation in Resource Applications and with the Coal and Synthetic Fuels Office in the policy office. Both of these offices were also involved in the production of NETS.

Other DOE participants, while in no sense neutral, did not have such well-defined missions. Resource Applications was concerned that the report be finished in a manner acceptable to all who had to concur on it. The Secretary's office was also primarily concerned that the report be completed. The policy office was concerned that the report reflect current DOE policies in energy transportation. The Energy Information Administration defined itself as a technical body and was concerned that the statistical basis for the analyses in the report be correct. Environment was involved to make sure that environmental impacts of energy transportation were included in the report. The General Counsel's office was responsible for seeing that statements made in the document were legally justifiable; it was also concerned about the impact of statements made in the report on cases in which it was involved. Nuclear Energy wanted to make sure that parts of the report dealing with the transport of nuclear materials be written in a "fair-minded" manner.

The Process

Formally, DOT had the major responsibility for the report as of May 1978. This included responsibility for hiring consultants to do the analyses that would be used in the report. DOE was supposed to participate in decisions about the scope of the analyses and the selection of the consultants. Each department was supposed to commit three people for one year to the project and to make available people with particular expertise as they were needed. In fact, DOT produced the first draft of the report with some help from people in DOE on specific topics. An internal DOT option paper written in January 1980 indicates that some people in that agency even considered releasing NETS as a report from the Secretary of Transportation rather than a joint DOE/DOT report.

The fact that DOT primarily had written the report was interpreted differently by people in the two agencies. In a letter sent from DOT to Resource Applications in DOE on April 24, 1980, that accompanied copies of the draft report, the writer expressed the feeling that most of the work was done and that DOE should now make comments on the report and send them to DOT. The DOT staff would then make the appropriate adjustments, everyone could concur on the report, and the process would be over. The letter indicated that comments were expected by May 5.

In the first DOE meeting about the report, held May 6, people expressed the opinion that they had been presented with a fait accompli, the content of which they did not like. People saw it as a forum for DOT positions that had left out any consideration of the DOE position on the same topics. As there had been earlier interactions between the two departments on several of these topics, ignorance was not a valid excuse. Some people expressed the opinion that the report was not salvageable and that they should not waste any more time on it. The strongest of these opinions was expressed by the participants from the Economic Regulatory Administration. The participants from Resource Applications took a more moderate stand, saying that a lot of work

had to be done, but that the report could be saved. Other participants were unsure about whether or not the report could be
saved but were willing to think about what saving it would
entail.

At this meeting the Economic Regulatory Administration participants suggested sending a memorandum to the Secretary
outlining the problems with the document, listing options for
what could be done with the report, and suggesting that DOE
withdraw from having anything to do with it. After a great deal
of talk about this possibility, the person in charge of the report
from Resource Applications prevailed upon the entire group to
write up specific comments about what was wrong with the
study as it now stood. The participants from the Economic Regulatory Administration volunteered to collect, combine, and con-
dense all the comments. Through this activity, they could set
the tone of the comments. This satisfied the need to do something without having a firm commitment to a course of action.

Whether a memo would be sent to the Secretary was left unresolved. However, because the suggestion had been made, the
staff-level participants in the process needed to advise their superiors of the possibility that this could happen. The meeting
thus resulted in both intradepartmental and intraoffice communications about the study.

During the period that these comments and memos were
being written, one of the staff members in the Economic Regulatory Administration called a staff member in the policy office
and suggested that that office take the lead in "trashing" the report. This way, he said, his office could go to the head of the
Economic Regulatory Administration and tell her that the policy
office was going to do this and that they should also. The staff
member in the policy office did not go along with this plan. Economic Regulatory Administration staff members may have made
this suggestion to other participants as well. If so, apparently no
one was amenable to the plan. This was the last heard of dropping the effort altogether.

On May 14, the assistant secretary responsible for the report
in DOT wrote to the assistant secretary responsible for the report in DOE. He stated that comments had been expected by
May 5. He gave a more detailed version of the schedule intended

for NETS, saying that interim deadlines would have to be met in order to keep this schedule. He stated his intention to direct his staff to work with DOE staff to agree on interim deadlines. This was the first formal indication that people in DOT recognized that producing a final draft of NETS would involve direct interaction with people in DOE, though the interaction referred to was still fairly minimal. The earlier letter contained the implicit assumption that a more customary process involving mostly indirect interaction (e.g., sending in comments) would take place. A few days after receiving this letter (May 19) the head of Resource Applications sent a memo to the heads of Policy and Evaluation, the Economic Regulatory Administration, the Energy Information Administration, and the Office of the General Counsel asking that each contribute one person full-time for three weeks to make the report acceptable to the Secretary.

On May 20, 24 pages of "preliminary comments" were finally sent from the office in DOE responsible for the report to the equivalent office in DOT. A memo accompanied the comments. The memo did two things. First, it softened the effect of the comments by stating that some of them were strongly worded and that they did not necessarily represent the view of DOE as a whole. Second, it indicated that direct interaction between staff members of the two departments was anticipated by stating that a DOE team was being put together and would soon be ready to meet with DOT representatives.

A week later the DOE team met. The study was divided into three sections, and leaders for each section were selected. The three sections represented the most problematic parts of the report: the overview, the data, and the chapter on coal transportation. The person from the office in Resource Applications who had been in charge of the May 6 meeting was a logical choice to lead the effort to revise the overview. The person from the Energy Information Administration was, similarly, an obvious choice for the data section. No one was as clearly suited to head the coal section. The person from Resource Applications wanted someone from the Economic Regulatory Administration to be in charge of this section. This made sense in two ways. This office had the strongest objection to what had been written in this chapter, and if someone from that office was responsible for revising that section, that person would be in a good position to make the desired changes. In addition, this office had been the most adamant about dropping the report altogether. Involving it in the process of altering NETS might decrease the likelihood that they would still favor that option. The staff members from the Economic Regulatory Administration present at this meeting, however, claimed to be too busy to become heavily involved in this activity. The representative from the General Counsel's office was another possibility, but he also asked that his involvement be kept to a minimum. The staff member from the policy office was then chosen to lead this section.

A couple of days later the policy staff member (now head of the coal section) met with the Energy Information Administration staff member (now head of the data section). The staff member from the Energy Information Administration had found a large discrepancy between the 1978 projections of coal supply and demand on which the NETS analysis had been based and the 1979 projections, which were scheduled to be released close to the same time that NETS would probably be released. This difference raised three concerns in relation to the NETS report. The first was whether or not this difference was large enough to affect the validity of the analyses used in NETS. The second was to identify the assumptions used in the 1978 model that had been changed in the 1979 version of the model and to determine whether these changes altered what could or should be said in the report. The third concern was how to fix up the report without completely redoing the analyses (which would be costly and time-consuming) so that readers would know that the authors were aware of and had taken into account the discrepancy.

The first joint DOE/DOT meeting to resolve the problems with NETS was held on Monday, June 2. A representative from the Secretary's office in DOE attended this meeting. Her presence was interpreted by other DOE participants as indicating that the Secretary felt this report was important and wanted it to be completed. The meeting began at 9:00 and continued until shortly before 12:00, then reconvened shortly after 1:00 and continued until 3:00. This was the pattern for the next four days. Most of the participants had some sort of task that they carried away at 3:00 to be completed by 9:00 the next morning. These might be to read an as-yet-unread section and prepare comments, to propose wording on a problematic section, or to check with one's superior to make sure that something was acceptable. Often parts of the DOE group would meet afterwards (this was, presumably, also true of the DOT group) to discuss what had gone on, what they liked and did not like, and what they would like to have happen in the next meeting. Sometimes specific issues would be discussed and there would be an effort to establish which features of an issue were important to one office or another (features that must be present for that office to sign off on the report) and which features were throwaways ("bargaining beans," as one person called them).

The size of the group expanded and contracted over the course of the week. More people were present for the general overview sections, and the fewest people were present for the petroleum, natural gas, and nuclear materials chapters. More people were present at the beginning and fewer people at the end of the four days. Normally there were about ten people; the largest number was twelve, and there were never fewer than six.

The participants in these meetings all sat around a table and went through the report page by page. For every page people were asked if they had any problems with it. Problems were raised and dealt with. With few exceptions the next page was not taken up until all the problems with the previous page had been resolved. The problems ranged from how to word and where to insert a caveat about the discrepancy between the 1978 and 1979 projections discussed earlier to proverbial arguments over "a" and "the." People became known for their idiosyncratic likes and dislikes. One person did not like the use of such words as "massive" and "tremendous." Another person wanted the details of every explanation included. A third person resisted the inclusion of any new tables. And so on.

By Thursday, June 5, all of the report had been read, discussed, and altered and was approvable, except the coal chapter. In fact, the coal chapter had not been part of this four-day effort, though there were a number of statements about coal in the general overview sections. By this time people were beginning to feel it was time for a break. Many of the participants had barely been in their offices for the past week, and when they had, they had been busy preparing for the next day's meeting. Other responsibilities were being neglected. Perhaps just as important, people were getting tired of the activity. It had been an intense and draining experience. The group determined to reconvene almost a week later—on Wednesday, June 11. As the most problematic portion of the study was yet to be discussed, some part of the days between meetings were to be spent preparing acceptable wordings for the currently unacceptable chapter.

During the period in which these meetings were going on, the assistant secretary of Resource Applications in DOE finally replied to the letter sent to her nearly a month earlier (May 14) from an assistant secretary in DOT. That letter had expressed some displeasure that DOE had not yet sent comments to DOT. The response stated that a DOE team had been assembled and was working closely with DOT representatives to revise the report. It also said that the process should be completed and comments issued by June 10. This response imposed a new deadline by saying that the process would be completed by June 10. It was left a little ambiguous, however, what exactly would happen by June 10. Since the process referred to, revising the report, involved making the document acceptable to both departments, there should be no need for comments once the process was completed. The letter made no mention of the comments that had already been sent, thus increasing the ambiguity about what the analysts were committed to do by June 10.

Prior to the next joint DOE/DOT meeting, a DOE-only meeting was held to discuss the problems everyone had with the coal chapter and to consider what changes people felt needed to be made. Rather than resulting in firm decisions about what should or should not be said, this meeting allowed people to express what was important to them and to other members of their offices. The basis for solidarity in the coming meeting was provided by the sense that if a particular phrasing was important to one person in the group, other people from DOE would support that wording.

Representatives from both DOE and DOT met again on June 11 as arranged. This was supposed to be the last meeting, and there had been some mention of completing the coal chapter that day. Seventeen people showed up for this meeting, including representatives from the Federal Railroad Administration and the General Counsel in DOT, neither of which had been represented in earlier meetings. The number of people present was an indicator of how many problems there were in this chapter. Though in earlier meetings the group had corrected more than one chapter per day (six chapters in four days), none of the other chapters had been considered nearly as problematic as this one. Not surprisingly, the group was not able to complete all the corrections in this one day.

The large number of participants may have been partially responsible for the fact that most of the discussions that day were carried on among small groups of people who specialized in the area being discussed. The whole group focused on the same topic only when the general sections on railroads and coal slurry pipelines were discussed. That the whole group was not needed to discuss most issues, coupled with the realization that the process was going to take longer than expected, contributed to the emergence of a new way of handling the process of writing this report. Parts of the chapter were parceled out to small groups made up of people who had an interest in the issue dealt with in a particular section. They were supposed to meet sometime after this meeting and negotiate wordings. By the end of the day, the sections on coal haul road financing, coal exports, the general financial condition of the railroads, the waterways, and coal by wire were all left to small groups. Coordinators for DOE and DOT were also specified to make sure that the work of the groups was read and approved by all participants.

Another spin-off occurred when the DOE participants in the group dealing with the financial condition of the railroads (from the Economic Regulatory Administration) said that they would like to have the DOT participants come up with the initial wording so that they could get back to work on other things. None of the DOT people involved in that group were attending the afternoon meeting. The suggestion was accepted by all who were there. In this way the small group was effectively dissolved and yet another method emerged for rewriting the report. This method was more like what had first been envisioned by the people in DOT, in which there would be no direct interaction between participants of the different organizational entities.

Each of the small groups quickly provided wording they found acceptable, with the exception of the group just discussed, dealing with the financial condition of the railroads. As requested, the DOT representatives sent wording to the Economic Regulatory Administration, but they did not carry through on their part until the representative from the Secretary's office who had been at the first NETS meeting called them to find out what was causing the delay. The delay ended with her call, and a statement acceptable to all participants was sent from the office in the Economic Regulatory Administration that afternoon. While one of the main differences between this and the other groups was the method used to get the work done, there are other factors that could also have caused the delay. For instance, several times during the NETS process the representatives from the Economic Regulatory Administration had claimed to be busy, and it is possible that the staff was occupied with other projects. It is also possible that they used delay as a strategy to increase the likelihood that they would get the wording they wanted.

The last NETS meeting was held on June 23. The main subject again was the coal chapter. This was also a time for bringing up any remaining problems with the rest of the report. It was not, however, a time to reopen issues that had already been resolved. By the end of the day all parts of the study had been approved by the working group.

In the next weeks the agreed-upon changes would be made so that a final draft of the report could be circulated for concurrence. Though the changes had been approved by the working group, the report still had to go through the formal concurrence process.

During this time a meeting of the DOE coal transportation group was called by the head of the Office of Energy Supply Transportation, who chaired this group. There was a great deal of overlap between the members of this group and the people who worked on NETS, and this meeting was intended primarily as a sort of debriefing after the NETS report-writing experience. Most of the meeting, however, focused on some news that one of the staff members from the Economic Regulatory Administration had brought. He said that while NETS was being written, another report, "Moving U.S. Coal to Export Markets," had been written, primarily by people in International Affairs in

DOE with help from DOT. This report contained many of the same statements that had been objectionable to the DOE staff in the first draft of NETS. The big news was that President Carter had taken this report to the recent economic summit meeting in Vienna at which energy issues had been discussed. This made many of the people at the meeting furious. It meant that, to the extent that coal transportation was discussed at the summit, the report taken provided the basis for the administration position. The people felt that since the president had taken the report, he had in some sense committed himself to the positions in it, and therefore all the work the NETS team had done to make sure that those positions seen as favoring the DOT perspective did not become administration policy had been preempted.

The process continued, however. The National Energy Transportation Study might not have as much influence as some of its authors had hoped, but that did not justify giving up on the report. The report had been requested by the president. As such, it was a part of the official responsibilities of the two departments involved, and, frankly, it would probably have taken more effort to stop the report at this point than to continue it.

A month after the last NETS meeting, the process of getting concurrence signatures began. A memorandum was sent from the assistant secretary of Resource Applications to the assistant secretaries and administrators of all the DOE offices that had to concur on the report. Since this was a formal communication, it was sent to the heads of the offices involved and then forwarded to the analysts. This process can produce miscommunication, though in this case it did not. (The report had been available informally to staff two days before, so most of the involved staff ended up with two copies of the report.) The memo asked that formal concurrence be submitted to the coordinating office no later than July 25. The report would then be submitted to the secretary's office for DOE endorsement. The memo arrived on July 22, allowing a little more than three days between the beginning of the formal concurrence process and the requested termination of the process.

The recommendation that the policy office concur on the NETS report went from the policy staff member through the assistant office director, the office director, and the deputy assistant secretary to the assistant secretary. While only the assistant secretary's signature was required, the document would not get to his office until the other people had approved it.

The assistant office director approved the report without hesitation. The office director asked the staff member to write an explanation of the major changes that had been made in the report. This was added to the memo that recommended concurrence. After this was done, he concurred. The memo, with the explanation and the report, then went to the deputy assistant secretary. He asked for two things. One was that the directors of the nuclear, natural gas, and oil offices within the policy office read and comment on the document. Until then only the coal office of policy had been involved. Second, he wanted a written summary of the report to replace the statement of major changes that had been written for the office director. The staff member wrote the summary and distributed the document to the office directors in the specified offices. The director of the natural gas office approved the report on the condition that some changes be made. The staff member called DOT to make sure that these changes could be made. The other two office directors approved the document with no changes. With this completed, the deputy assistant secretary concurred on the document. As the staff member waited to find out what the assistant secretary would need before he could concur, word came from the deputy assistant secretary's office that, in this case, his signature stood for the assistant secretary's. Thus, the report had the approval of the policy office. This concurrence took longer than the three days allotted—final approval was granted on July 31.

After all the relevant DOE offices had concurred on the report, it was sent to the Secretary's offices in both DOE and DOT. Both Secretaries signed it, and it was ready for publication on August 4, 1980. The release was then delayed until some other energy transportation announcements could be made. "The National Energy Transportation Study: A Preliminary Report to the President" was released September 30, 1980.

Two Other Cases

While NETS is a good illustration of many features important to understanding report writing, no single case can cover the full range of circumstances in the process. To give a sense of this range, two other cases are introduced and briefly summarized here. They are presented in detail in Appendix A.

Coal Slurry Pipeline Testimony

Every year since its inception the Department of Energy was asked to testify before Congress on various bills concerning coal slurry pipelines.* In general, the legislation concerned granting the right of federal eminent domain for the pipelines, which the department had always favored. Every year analysts from several offices in the department had met to discuss the particulars of that year's proposed legislation and to decide what should be included in the testimony.

In 1981 the process changed as a result of the Reagan administration's requirement of a unified administration position. Whereas in the past testimony was coordinated within departments and departments might give contradicting testimony, this year testimony had to be coordinated across departments.

The original draft of the testimony was written by analysts in the White House in cooperation with the Secretary of the Interior. It was circulated to the Departments of Energy, Interior, Justice, and Transportation and the Interstate Commerce Commission. Analysts in these organizations responded. They never met, but wrote responses that were shepherded by their bosses or higher officials to the White House staff and to meetings that sometimes included several cabinet members. The analysts developed better information and better ways of presenting their arguments over the course of several drafts, but they were not involved in making procedural claims.

Eventually, the president decided that the unified position the administration would take would oppose granting federal eminent domain. The arguments supporting granting the right were taken out of the testimony, though some of the concerns about not granting the right were left in. For instance, the Department of Energy analysts had raised the concern that without federal

---

*A coal slurry pipeline is a way of transporting coal. The coal is ground very fine and mixed with water so that it can be pumped through a pipeline in much the same way that oil is. Once the coal has been transported, the water is removed, and the coal is ready to be used.

eminent domain the railroads would be able to block the development of slurry pipelines through the state legislatures. The president's memorandum to Secretary of the Interior James Watt, in which he stated his decision, and the final testimony presented to Congress by Secretary Watt included that concern and called for a group to be set up to ensure that did not happen. In fact, the president's memorandum used the same wording that had originated in the Department of Energy.

Railroad Revenue Adequacy

The legislature passed the Staggers Rail Act in 1980. Implementation of this act required establishing several regulations about such issues as what constitutes an adequate revenue level. The Interstate Commerce Commission (ICC) was responsible for the regulations. Establishing a regulation involves, first, posting a notice of proposed rulemaking in the Federal Register. Then those interested in the rule can comment on it. The regulatory agency takes these comments into consideration in determining what the final regulation is.

This case concerns the Department of Energy's (DOE) efforts to file comments on the ICC's proposed rule about railroad revenue adequacy. The three offices involved were from the Economic Regulatory Administration, the General Counsel's Office, and the policy office. They had just filed comments on another proposed rulemaking for the same act. This experience had involved considerable conflict, as had earlier, similar interactions between these offices, even those among different analysts. The source of the conflict was partly the Economic Regulatory Administration's strong stand on protecting the interest of the coal consumer against the avarice of the railroads. Having to coordinate with other parts of the DOE inevitably watered down this stand. To avoid this, the Economic Regulatory Administration staff tried to have more control over the process.

By common consent the Economic Regulatory Administration was the appropriate office to have the lead on writing these comments. Thus, they already had a fair amount of control, since they always wrote the first draft. They attempted to increase their control in two ways. First, they asked the other offices to concur before the paper was written, by sending a memorandum to the other offices requesting permission to file comments. They would then interpret this as permission to file whatever they wrote. Eventually, the other offices caught on to this strategy and refused to sign the memorandum. The second strategy to gain control was to send the draft comments to the other offices a day or two before the deadline, leaving other analysts little time to make changes if they wanted the DOE to file comments.

In this case, the analysts from the Office of the General Counsel and the policy office tried to fight back. They hired a consultant, went to talk with an analyst at the ICC, and eventually wrote their own version of the comments. Interactions between these two analysts and the analysts in the Economic Regulatory Administration were very strained, with analysts in the Economic Regulatory Administration refusing to talk first to the analyst from the policy office and then to the analyst from the Office of the General Counsel. During a meeting one of the Economic Regulatory Administration analysts called the Office of the General Counsel analyst an idiot, and she then refused to talk with anyone from that office. Throughout this time drafts moved among the analysts, and just before the deadline they agreed on comments to file.

Summary

These three cases illustrate the broad range of circumstances under which papers are written. They differ in the reasons for writing the papers, in the combinations and numbers of actors, and in the interests that are of primary concern.

The papers differ in their origins. The first paper was a report from the departments to the president, required as part of legislation passed by Congress. In the second instance, the department was asked by Congress to testify about a bill the legislature was considering. The paper also was presented to an upper-level executive branch decision-making body and the president as they deliberated about the position the administration should take on this issue. The third consisted of comments to the Interstate Commerce Commission on regulations it had proposed. The commission was required to make rules defining terms and procedures for legislation passed by Congress. The Department of Energy did not have to file comments, although there was substantial precedent for doing so.

The three instances vary in the combination of the offices and departments represented and in the number of actors involved. The first paper was a joint Department of Energy and Department of Transportation paper, involving several offices from each of these departments. The paper was written by a core of eight people, but sometimes as many as seventeen people were involved. The second had a large cast of characters including representatives of the White House, the Departments of Interior, Justice, Transportation, and Energy and the Interstate Commerce Commission. It is impossible to say how many people were involved since the analysts never interacted directly with one another. The third involved three offices and four analysts from within the Department of Energy.

The three cases begin to illustrate the variety of interests that are engaged in the process of report writing. While the substance of the paper is always the manifest concern, the interests brought to bear on the process are often less technical and more procedural or organizational. Concern over substance appears to be the most straightforward in the slurry pipeline case. However, the whole episode occurred because of a concern about presenting a united administration opinion to the Congress. There was also considerable debate and speculation over which department would give the testimony. In the NETS case some of the concern over substance really involved consistency or being able to obtain concurrence. In the railroad revenue adequacy case, the concern about substance was transformed into and nearly subsumed by a fight over process.

Despite these differences, the three cases illustrate the fundamental similarities in the process. They all involve analysts from different offices who represent different interests. The cases show how the analysts use the papers to negotiate for their interests, whether they are substantive, procedural, or some combination of these.* The analysts are constrained in this process

---

*These interests are defined not only by the analysts' offices but also by the analysts themselves. Thus, it is difficult always to tell the difference between defending bureaucratic turf and defending interests. The former is, at least, often cloaked in terms of the latter.

by the demand that the paper be signed by all the offices on the concurrence list. Despite conflict and threats to withdraw from writing the paper, a signed report almost always results from the process—indeed, though it must occur, in one and one-half years I never witnessed nor heard of a paper-writing process that did not result in a completed and signed report.

Conclusion

These three descriptions capture the essence of how bureaucratic analysts produce papers. The process requires substantive expertise as well as the ability to negotiate. The analysts work within considerable constraints. Some are imposed by the specifics of the request for information. The concurrence list accompanying the paper and the amount of disagreement that exists among the offices on the list impose additional constraints. The analysts are also restricted by the interests of the office they represent. As illustrated in the preceding cases, the exact working out of each process depends upon the details of the context.

CHAPTER 5

Tasks That Contribute to Report Writing

BUREAUCRATIC ANALYSTS produce information primarily by writing papers. A description of this process, however, gives only a partial view of their work. Analysts often participate in a much less involved manner than portrayed in the cases in Chapter 4. In addition, they often perform tasks other than writing that prepare them to be effective participants in paper writing. These include knowing about the issue, creating new information about the issue, understanding the organization's position on the issue, and establishing a role that allows one to influence the papers that are being written. There is substantial overlap among these four, and one activity may accomplish more than one task. For the sake of clarity they are discussed and illustrated separately in this chapter, and the contribution of each to the report-writing process—and particularly to the production of interpretations in reports—is explored.

The activities portrayed in this chapter are mostly those of five bureaucratic analysts from one division of the policy office, the Office of Coal and Synthetic Fuels. Each chose the issue he or she would talk about; each then reported what tasks had been performed relevant to the issue every week for twelve weeks (the observation period, December 1980–March 1981). This chapter introduces each of the analysts and the issue she or he chose to talk about. Examples from their reports are used to show how the work they do supports and influences paper writing. Their reports are recorded in full in Appendix B.

The Analysts

Gregory and Marvin both dealt with issues of gasification and liquefaction. Gregory was in the midst of writing a three-part report on the production and marketing of methanol. This report took up most of his time, so he reported on his activities that related to it. Marvin's activities were more diffuse. This may have been, in part, because he had an operation scheduled during the observation period. He spent time supporting Gregory's efforts, catching up on information relevant to his issues, and reviewing unsolicited proposals for research.

Anne reported on the issue of impact assistance. Her office was not a "major player" in this issue—those most involved were in another part of the Department of Energy and in the Department of Agriculture. As a result, her office was often not on the concurrence list for papers dealing with this issue, and because of her peripheral position Anne had to work at just finding out what other people were doing on the issue. She also tried to convince her superiors that the office should become more involved in the issue.

Edna reported on her activities having to do with the socioeconomic impacts of synthetic fuel production. She was trying to obtain funding to hire a consultant to write about specific cases. She also interacted a number of times with other analysts in the Department of Energy and in other departments who had responsibility for the same issue.

Daniel reported on his responsibilities in the area of coal leasing. He commented on a number of reports that examined questions arising from the federal government's programs to lease land for mining.

Minimal Engagement in Report Writing

A great deal of conflict and confusion characterizes the writing of many papers. This makes it nearly impossible to finish the paper without face-to-face meetings in which people can hash out their disagreements and make clear what they mean. The cases in Chapter 3 all entail some form of meetings to resolve issues.* This is not an odd state of affairs, but it is also not the only one. There is sometimes less conflict over the papers or more common ground among the analysts and offices responsible for them. In these cases meetings are often foregone, and papers are simply sent out for comments and, later, approval. In fact, this is the way the National Energy Transportation Study process began. It was only when it became apparent that there was a lot of disagreement that the process changed.

Often the first draft of a report is written by one person or group of people within the office that has the lead for that paper. The draft is sent to the relevant analysts (mostly those whose offices are on the concurrence list) for comments. The comments are then used to revise the draft. This process may occur several times. Later drafts may be quickly prepared and recirculated, or they may take months. When people in the lead office think that they have responded adequately to comments, they send the report out for concurrence. At this point the analyst with responsibility for the issue writes a memorandum to his or her boss either recommending or not recommending concurrence. Memoranda may also have to be written to people in higher offices.

Gregory's and Daniel's activities provide examples of this process from different sides: Gregory on the sending side; Daniel on the receiving side. At the beginning of the observation period, Gregory sent Phase I of the report on methanol to a wide array of people. Toward the end of the observation period he received comments from these people. Gregory and his consultants would then revise the report, taking the comments into consideration. Eventually, it would be sent out for concurrence.

Most recipients of the report were people in the Department of Energy whose offices would have to approve the report at some point. However, Gregory also sent it to two people who no longer worked for the government, because, he said, "until recently they were in the department, working on methanol, and they had a lot of expertise in the area." His asking for comments from people who did not have to concur shows that he was con-

---

*In the slurry pipeline case, face-to-face meetings did not take place among the analysts but did at higher levels.

cerned not just with gaining approval, but also with improving the quality of the information. The primary purpose of this paper was to gather and analyze information, unlike papers for testimony before Congress or comments to a regulatory commission, which primarily present the position of the organization. This emphasis on information tends to encourage the solicitation of comments from experts who do not have to approve the report. This kind of report is discussed in more detail below.

Daniel was on the commenting side of this process. During the observation period, he commented on four reports and recommended concurrence on them. His activities illustrate some of the complications of this process. In one instance he confronted difficulties in making sure that he was included in the commenting process. In another case the authors of the paper took so long to produce it that the person who commented on it originally had left. Daniel had different objections to it. He was torn between raising his objections to certain assumptions in the paper and meeting the expectations of his superiors.

The first instance involved a report on coal leasing goals. Daniel was, apparently unintentionally, left out of the commenting loop some of the time. The report first came out several months before the three-month observation period. It went to a staff member in another part of the policy office who commented on it and sent it back. The report was revised and sent out for comment again in September. This time it came to Daniel. As he read the report, he noticed references to earlier comments indicating that, though he had never seen the report before, this was not the first draft. Daniel called the people who had sent out the report and found out who had made the earlier comments for policy. He then called that policy staff member, and they coordinated their responses for the September version of the report.

The latest version of the report, which came out during Week 2 of the observation period, was sent neither to Daniel nor to the other policy staff member who had been involved. Instead, it went directly to the office of the assistant secretary, the head of the policy office several hierarchical levels removed from both Daniel and the other policy staff member. Daniel found out about this from the person who had sent out the report. He called the assistant secretary's office to ask that it be sent to him. He and the other policy staff member again coordinated their comments.

Another example of the complications that can come up in the commenting and concurring process were related to the final report on coal production goals. Daniel first saw the report when it was nearly final. Earlier versions of the report had been circulated in the policy office but at that time had been the responsibility of another person in Daniel's office. She had since left the office, and the report had become Daniel's responsibility. This created an uncomfortable situation for him. He had some fairly serious disagreements with the assumptions used in the model that generated the goals. If he had commented on the report when it first came out, these objections would probably have been addressed. At this point, however, the writers of the report had already responded to comments and thought that the paper had been adequately revised. They were sending it out this time for concurrence, not for more comments. Thus, Daniel could either raise his objections as a reason not to concur, or he could recommend concurrence. He did not feel that it would be appropriate for him to recommend not concurring. As he said, "To not concur for theoretical reasons does not cut ice with my superiors. This is a pragmatic office, and we work with the best we have. Not concurring on purely theoretical grounds is not an alternative. Shortstopping a process on purely theoretical grounds is against the department's objectives."

Through this process of sending reports out for comments, then, bureaucratic analysts contribute to report writing without as much involvement as portrayed in the cases in Chapter 3. They give and receive comments that alter the substance of the reports. They also influence their superiors' decisions about whether to concur on the reports.

The processes of commenting and concurring are linked substantively and procedurally. The comments provide information about how to revise the paper so that it can be approved. The commenting process also provides some reassurance to the authors of the paper that their work will not be in vain. Writers of a paper are expected to ask for and respond to comments. As Daniel's experience showed, however, they are not expected to continue responding indefinitely. The norm may be stated as "speak now or forever hold your peace."

Activities Supporting Paper Writing

Bureaucratic analysts perform a number of tasks that do not involve engaging with other analysts to produce information, but that do support and affect their participation in report writing. This section looks at the tasks of keeping track of an issue, gathering and analyzing information about the issue, developing ideas about how to interpret the issue, and even establishing the right to participate in papers written about the issue. None of these tasks is straightforward, and analysts confront numerous problems in performing them.

Knowing the Issue

Analysts have to know about the issue(s) they have responsibility for. This means keeping up with both technological and political developments. Without such information it is very hard to be effective. The information is important for two reasons. First, some of it will have effects on what is appropriate or inappropriate to include in a paper. Second, it provides a means for analysts to signal how much they know and how current their knowledge is. How much current information an analyst has is a kind of test for how much the analyst really knows about what he or she is doing. Thus, even if the developments are not particularly important, knowing about them may be.

The analysts gather this information in a variety of ways; specific examples cited in parentheses refer to Appendix B. For technical information they read trade journals (Daniel, weeks 7, 11) and reports (Marvin, weeks 7, 8, 9; Gregory, weeks 1, 5, 8, 12), and they talk with experts (Marvin, weeks 9, 11). They also visit research and production facilities and discuss development plans with analysts from industry and government. (Though none of the five analysts participated in the latter activities during the observation period, I participated in and/or observed all of these activities over the year and a half I was with DOE.)

The most common source for political information is other bureaucratic analysts who deal with the same issue (Edna, weeks

4, 5; Anne, weeks 1, 5, 12; Daniel, week 5). Analysts also learn about what is happening in their department or in the administration as a whole from their bosses or other department officials (Daniel, weeks 10, 11). Other political information comes from members of legislative staffs and lobbying groups.

Analysts may have problems obtaining information about the issue(s) they have responsibility for. Information is neither automatically available nor particularly systematic in its sources. Sometimes it flows through superiors and traditional organizational lines. Sometimes, however, information is withheld or hard to obtain. For instance, though Anne was responsible for the impact assistance issue, she was not invited to a meeting in which some aspects of dealing with this issue were discussed (week 1), and she was not sent a copy of the legislation another member of the department was writing (week 5).

Sometimes information is found in unexpected places or gathered in unconventional ways. Serendipity often plays a role. Gregory found a report that was relevant to his study when he was talking with people about other matters (Gregory, week 1). He saved $10,000 by incorporating it into his study. Luck also played a role in the incident related earlier in which Daniel found that he had not been included in the commenting process.

Other times information is simply not available. Marvin found this when he tried to provide Gregory with the cost breakdown of the production of gasoline for automobiles. He talked with representatives of several organizations, both public and private, all with expertise in energy and economics. He found that none of them had much information (Marvin, week 9).

Creating New Information

Analysts also develop information on their own. They gather data, analyze them, and write information reports. These reports have a dual role: they are negotiated agreements, subject to the same constraints as other papers, but they also make new information available for future use. Most papers, of course, contain some new information, but for information reports, presenting new data is the primary objective. The paper that Gregory was working on was an information report. He and the consultants working for him might spend months, even years, gathering and analyzing data and developing new models for understanding the barriers to methanol production. Thus, the report would change the amount and type of information available for future reports on methanol. Edna's efforts to find funding for her project could also result in such a report.

These efforts to develop information bring with them administrative complications as well as substantive ones. Analysts must have support and approval of their efforts. Money must come from somewhere to support the costs of the report. Usually—but not always—this money comes from the organization the analyst works for. Edna solicits support from other organizations for her study (Edna, weeks 1, 5). Even Gregory, whose study is well supported by his office, uses some money from a contract granted to another office in the department (Gregory, week 5).

Approval, generally, is closely tied to the provision of money. Thus, Gregory spent much of his time during the first half of the observation period working out details of the contract with his boss, the technical advisor, and the procurement officer. He also carefully prepared briefings for his boss, on whose approval the project was contingent (Gregory, weeks 6, 7).

Understanding the Organization's
Position on an Issue

Bureaucratic analysts develop ideas about how to interpret issues. To be effective in the paper-writing process, they have to have ideas about the interests of their organizations and what the officials in the organization consider to be the appropriate grounds for concurrence or nonconcurrence. In an earlier example, for instance, Daniel commented that though he had theoretical objections to a paper, he would not use them to recommend nonconcurrence because that would not be acceptable to his superiors. Analysts develop this kind of sense through interactions with their bosses and other officials. Some of the interactions take place around writing papers. In the National Energy Transportation Study, for instance, the analysts in the policy office had to provide different kinds of information to different superiors before gaining approval of the report. This exercise gave the analyst a sense of what each official's general perspectives were and what interests mattered to each of them. Gregory also experienced this kind of interaction when he was writing the contract for Phase II of his report.* In his meetings with his boss and with the technical advisor, each made suggestions for changes in the contract and the scope of work. After the contract was written, Gregory and his consultants continued to give his boss briefings on their work, and the boss continued to give them comments and directions.

There are many other opportunities for analysts to develop a sense of the appropriate way to think about an issue. During staff meetings bosses often report on what higher officials of the department are concerned about. Analysts may talk to their bosses about specific assignments they have been given or papers they have to write. Written communication is also an important way for analysts to find out more about their organization's position. Memoranda reviewed by officials are often returned with questions or comments that give analysts a new or different appreciation for the perspective of their superiors. These written communications may be particularly useful, since they often spell out details that have been discussed only in vague terms.

Analysts also learn from one another. They relate their experiences to one another, particularly great successes and failures. One analyst, for instance, talked about how he and another analyst had "gotten their asses in a sling" for taking a particular stand that the deputy assistant secretary did not like (field notes, 4/29/80). This story communicated a message about both who should be attended to and what particular stand was dangerous to take.

Analysts are not just passive representatives of the office's positions, but also help to develop ways of thinking about issues by defining what they think are relevant concerns. Managers rely on the analysts as the experts to perform this function. A common approach is to write a memorandum or a short paper that discusses what features of an issue need consideration. Three of the analysts had written such papers for an internal policy document (Marvin, week 1; Anne, week 1; Daniel, week 1).

*He presumably had a similar experience with Phase I, but I did not observe it.

Edna wrote such a paper for an intradepartmental committee that deals with her issue (Edna, weeks 5, 6). She called it a "problems paper" because it discussed the features of the issue that she and her peers saw as potential problems. Analysts may also influence this process in more informal ways during staff meetings or in conversations with their bosses.

Edna's activities also illustrate another way of influencing what is seen as relevant to an issue. She sent a memorandum to the Assistant General Counsel for Legislation in which she suggested a modification in the Defense Economic Adjustment Act. This act provides assistance for areas of the country that are burdened by the amount of land devoted to defense-related activities and was coming up for consideration during that congressional session. Edna's memorandum suggested that the DOE push for the act to be redefined to include areas that are similarly burdened by energy-related activities. Through this type of action analysts not only come to understand the organization's position, but also contribute to developing it.

Analysts write and talk about the issues they are responsible for. They receive feedback from peers and superiors. They obtain information about what positions have been taken in the past and where officials currently stand on both specific issues and general principles. They also influence the organizational position. Through these actions they gain an understanding of the interests they represent and the appropriate positions to take in the paper-writing processes they are involved in.

Establishing a Role in the Issue Network

Analysts work to establish their positions among other analysts who deal with an issue. Even though they are given responsibility for an issue, they do not necessarily have the authority they need to make a difference or even to be included in writing papers on the issue. Anne was responsible for an issue for which her office was not considered very important; it was not on the concurrence list for many actions on the issue. As a result, Anne, as a representative of the policy office, had little power. She was not invited to attend meetings. She was dependent on other offices for important information about the development of the issue she was responsible for. She tried to change this situation by convincing her superiors in the policy office that the office should play a larger role in this area.

Sometimes analysts have problems establishing their roles because, though the office is on the concurrence list, it is not clear which analysts should represent that office. This was the case in one of the papers Daniel was involved in, described above. The paper first went to one analyst and then to another because the analysts had overlapping responsibilities. There are many ways to work this out. The two could vie with one another for the responsibility either formally or informally. Formal means would involve asking their bosses to resolve the conflict. Informally, each could try to persuade others involved with the issue that he or she is the relevant expert. In this case, the two analysts avoided conflict and simply shared the commenting responsibilities.

To be effective, analysts need to be included in the network that deals with the issue they have responsibility for. Generally, they are included because their offices are on the concurrence list, but there is more to establishing one's role. An analyst's expertise and willingness to work with other analysts can increase his or her acceptance. This is important to analysts because greater acceptance leads to more sharing of information. For instance, if Daniel is accepted as an expert on coal leasing, then when something related to coal leasing comes up, people will call to find out what he knows and what he thinks. Through these calls, Daniel will find out about the action and what other people think are the facts and concerns relevant to it. He, then, has more information to share and there is even more reason for people to call him. Daniel's expertise multiplies (Weiner, 1976). Thus, by being established in his role he is in a position to increase both his expertise and his acceptance. Both are useful in the process of report writing.

Effects on Report Writing

Through the performance of these tasks bureaucratic analysts contribute directly and indirectly to the report-writing process. Report writing is never far removed from these tasks and is affected by them. Primarily, the tasks enable the analysts to influence the facts and concerns represented in a paper in two ways. First, they better prepare analysts to promote the organization's position. Some of the tasks help them better to understand the organization's position. Others increase the quantity and quality of information they have to support the position. Second, the tasks allow the analysts to influence who is involved in writing papers. Efforts to redefine issues and to establish roles both have this potential.

When analysts comment on papers, they change the facts and concerns contained in them. Daniel, for instance, tried to influence the assumptions used in models that were the basis for papers he commented on. Marvin had a similar influence when he commented on and promoted certain research proposals. His actions were likely to affect not only current papers but future ones as well. The research proposals he supported would produce more information that could be used to argue for positions in future papers.

When analysts are in charge of writing a paper, they obviously have even more control over the concerns represented in the paper. Gregory had a great deal of influence on the topics covered in the paper he was in charge of. For instance, because he could use the existing report that he found, some of the money for his own report was freed up, and he chose to spend it on increasing the coverage of regulatory aspects of methanol production. Such a choice influences what type of information is available in the future.

Bureaucratic analysts also influence paper writing by increasing the quantity and quality of information available when they gather and analyze their own data. Gregory's methanol report had already resulted in new information on methanol production. This would continue if Phases II and III were completed. Similarly, if Edna's proposed study was ever funded, it would increase the amount of information available for making claims about the socioeconomic impacts of synthetic fuel production. Marvin increased the quality of information when he updated the crude oil price assumptions for Gregory's report. These efforts are not particularly dramatic, but they make a difference. When more and better factual information is available to support the interests analysts represent, it is harder to refute the claims they make.

Developing ideas about how to interpret an issue and establishing one's role in an issue area help analysts to redefine the issue they work on. Redefinition can mean changing who has control over and who is involved in the issue. Edna's efforts to convince the Assistant General Counsel for Legislation that the Defense Economic Adjustment Act should include "energy-impacted" as well as "defense-impacted" areas is a good example of redefining an issue. Anne also tried to redefine her issue when she sought to convince people that impact assistance is more policy-relevant than it has been considered before. At the same time a member of the program office of the Department of Energy was attempting to convince people that impact assistance is more of an energy issue and less of an agriculture issue.

Changing who is involved in writing on an issue necessarily changes the contents of the resulting reports. If the Defense Economic Adjustment Act were to be amended as Edna suggested, such issues as the comparison of defense-impacted areas with energy-impacted areas would have to be considered. If the policy office becomes more involved in impact assistance issues, then papers will reflect more concern with policy consistency and with the specific position the policy office takes on the issue.

Conclusion

Many of the tasks that bureaucratic analysts perform as part of their responsibilities for an issue influence report writing by influencing the ability of an analyst to promote a particular way of thinking about an issue and to argue for it effectively. The more information analysts have, the more likely they are to be able to influence the content of a paper. The acquisition and creation of information also influences the interpretation process. In addition, information is one of the primary sources of a bureaucratic analyst's power. The more information an analyst has, the more power he or she has to influence both how a problem is perceived and who should be involved in solving it. Gathering more or different information than is readily available may alter both how the problem is defined and who is involved in the process of producing solutions. Changing who participates in the report-writing process may have broad-ranging effects on what issues are raised and how they are resolved. Different people perceive their responsibilities differently and make different assessments of what is important and what is not. In these ways, the substance of reports is influenced by the work bureaucratic analysts do.

CHAPTER 6

The Work of Bureaucratic Analysts

M E L T S N E R (1976) has shown that analysts working in the bureaucracy have a fair amount of latitude in the roles they play. He points out that they can choose to place more or less emphasis on the analytical and the political aspects of their jobs. By so doing, they become more or less technical and more or less entrepreneurial in their orientation to their work.

While bureaucratic analysts do have and exercise these choices, there are also considerable constraints on the roles they play. The work they do is substantively demanding and procedurally complicated. They are asked to be experts in one or more areas. They also practice this expertise in a context that is very complicated. The most notable complications arise in their relations to their assigned responsibilities, in their relations to hierarchical superiors, in their relations to the interests they defend, and in their relations to peers who work on the same issues. Appropriate behavior in these areas is not clearly defined. However, the way their work is organized provides fairly specific opportunities to excel in the work and to distinguish oneself as a bureaucratic analyst. These opportunities act as constraints on what analysts do.

The Constraints of Responsibility

As we have seen in the last two chapters, analysts are generally assigned to cover broad issue areas and are responsible for all tasks relevant to that issue. This broad responsibility creates complexity in the role of bureaucratic analysts. Having responsibility for being an expert on an issue is a potentially infinite demand. Being such an expert includes understanding the technical, political, social, and economic aspects of the issue. It also includes keeping abreast of the latest developments in all these areas. Even being aware of all the bureaucratic actions relevant to an issue is a very large demand—such actions may be taking place in many different offices throughout the bureaucracy.

Clearly, bureaucratic analysts must make choices about what they attend to. Of course, this is a problem for virtually any professional. The form it takes for bureaucratic analysts is similar to the form it takes for university professors. There are certain tasks that must be done. For professors teaching courses falls in this category. For bureaucratic analysts it includes writing papers and providing information specifically requested by their hierarchical superiors. In both cases, this level of activity fulfills the minimum work obligations. In both cases, however, it is rare to see only this minimal level of work. The respect of one's peers and hierarchical superiors and opportunities for promotions and better jobs require more active engagement in work. In the case of university professors a program of research is the most common means of engaging more actively in work. Bureaucratic analysts can distinguish themselves by extending and expanding their minimum work in two ways. One is to pursue problems that arise in the course of fulfilling tasks that have been assigned. The other is to try to expand the tasks that are considered part of their responsibilities.

One of the striking features of the way analysts work is the persistence with which they confront problems that emerge. Though they may grumble, they do not take the easy way out. Daniel, for instance, when he realized that another analyst had commented on the paper he received, could have just sent it to that analyst to comment on again. He could have commented on it and not worried about who commented on it before or afterwards. Either of these options would have been easier than what he did.

Similarly, Marvin could have let Gregory continue to use four-year-old figures for the crude oil price assumptions in the methanol report. Instead, he thought "the report would be better" if he updated the figures. This effort involved doing some preliminary work, talking with economists in two private firms to compare the numbers he arrived at, having the numbers reviewed by offices inside and outside the department, and gaining the approval of his boss.

Anne was often not given information about the issue she was responsible for. She could have given up or refused to continue until relations were worked out at a higher level. However, she kept trying. She called people and tried to put together the pieces of information she received so that she knew as much as possible.

These efforts are not particularly heroic, but they are consistent. The examples could be multiplied indefinitely. While analysts clearly do not rise to every challenge, they do persistently confront the problems that arise in fulfilling their responsibilities.

They also go beyond confronting problems to fulfill their responsibilities. They try to expand their responsibilities. They try to become more involved in more aspects of the issue they are responsible for. They generate new projects. They try to take on responsibility for more issues.

Gregory's methanol report and Edna's efforts to write a report on the socioeconomic impact of synthetic fuel production are both good examples of analysts expanding the work they have to do. These reports are not a part of what is normally expected of the analysts. In fact, Edna was having a hard time obtaining the funding and approval for her report. Both analysts chose to go beyond what was expected of them.

Anne's activities provide another example. She tried to convince her superiors that the policy office should be more involved in impact assistance. If this happened, she would have much more work to do. Anne also related an example of another analyst who was trying to expand her responsibilities. This analyst was in another part of the department that was quite involved in impact assistance but not as involved as she wanted to be. She shared her responsibilities for this issue with another part of the Department of Energy and with the Department of Agriculture. Anne reported that this analyst was writing memoranda and proposing legislation to consolidate the impact assistance programs into the Department of Energy and within the department in her office.

Again, the examples could be multiplied indefinitely. Analysts often make efforts to increase the amount of work they do. Some of these look like standard "turf fights." Others are less oriented to control over the issue and more to increasing the information available about the issue or increasing the arenas in which the issue is considered.

While bureaucratic analysts could choose not to engage their work so vigorously, they would also be choosing to forgo the respect of their hierarchical superiors and peers and the career opportunities associated with such respect. This choice was exceedingly rare among the analysts observed for this study and tended, in fact, to be made largely by analysts who were both very alienated and nearing retirement. Others who were either less alienated or younger tended to work very hard. They often worked very long days and weekends and took work home with them. This was considered neither unusual nor onerous; most of the analysts liked working hard. As one said, "This office is busy right now. If not, it would be depressing" (interview 18).

The Constraints of Paper Writing

Since much of what bureaucratic analysts do is either directly or indirectly related to writing papers, the demands of this work play a large part in defining their roles. Only the minimum demands are absolute. However, the tendency to play similar roles is strong. At the least, bureaucratic analysts are expected to make sure that positions their office has taken on particular issues are represented in papers concerning those issues. This could mean that the analysts are told by their bosses what position to defend and that they simply relay the message that the position must be contained in the paper. In general, however, the role played by bureaucratic analysts in paper writing is much more complex.

Analysts do represent their offices and the positions supported by their offices. However, they are not simply mouthpieces. They are also experts who generally know more about the specific details of the issue that is the subject of the report than do any of their hierarchical superiors. Thus, they not only represent what their bosses want to have in a report, but they also have the responsibility of informing and persuading their bosses about the proper position for the office to take. Sometimes this involves dissuading their bosses from previous positions, but often their bosses rely on them to propose positions that the organization should take.

Opportunities to propose new positions sometimes arise because the organization has not previously taken a position on the issue. That may happen either because the issue is new or because the organization's involvement in the issue is new. Legislative, regulatory, political, or administrative changes may create new issues and new involvements. While most issues have been dealt with to some extent and the analysts are often constrained by what has been included in past papers, new questions are often raised, even on a topic that has been covered many times. These new questions provide opportunities for analysts to contribute to the positions of their organization. If bureaucratic analysts operated only as mouthpieces, the organization would lose the value of the expertise the analyst has in the issue area.

The analysts' role as expert also influences relations with other analysts. At one level the relations among analysts are adversarial, and they are intent on gaining concessions from one another on the substance of the paper. At another level, however, they often recognize one another as experts with valid points to make about the substance of the paper. They learn from one another and may develop different ideas about the appropriate position for their organization based on what they have learned.

The relationship among analysts goes beyond simply exchanging analytical points of view and is often quite interdependent. Analysts often work with each other time and again and expect these relationships to continue in the future. When they are working on a paper, they may spend much more time with one another than they do with the people in their own offices. They also depend on each other for important factual information and for keeping abreast of the latest developments concerning the issue they have responsibility for. Maintaining an interdependent relationship helps analysts do their work well. They have ready access to lots of information; they can often inform their bosses ahead of time when their issue is going to need attention; they may even be able to reach agreements about the substance of papers more easily. There is, of course, always the danger that the interdependent relationship will take precedence over the need to represent one's office.

Summary

The role of bureaucratic analysts is in no way straightforward. They are given assignments, but the expectations of their role go substantially beyond simply fulfilling these assignments. They are representatives of their offices and hierarchical superiors, but they are also advisors to their superiors. They defend the interests of their offices but also create and refine these interests. They are adversaries of analysts from other offices, but they also depend on them for critical information and cooperation.

The chapters in Part II provide background information about what bureaucratic analysts do. The way they produce information, the types of tasks they perform, and the complexities of their role all provide clues to understanding more about how analysts influence the process of issue interpretation in policy making. Part III explores these clues.

Contribution to Policy Making

CHAPTER 7

Rationality, Interpretation, and Inventories

THE BUREAUCRATIC ANALYSTS in this study and many observers of the policy process believe that what bureaucratic analysts do either is or ought to be consistent with the rational, or problem-solving, model presented in Chapter 2.* This means that they expect the behavior to contribute directly to the policy-making process by providing solutions to policy problems (Healy, 1986; Schneider, Stevens, and Tornatzky, 1982; Torgerson, 1986a). Students of decision making have noted that this is often an unrealistic expectation, and many have observed that it is also seldom met (Bozeman, 1986; Lindblom and Cohen, 1979; Lynn, 1978; Weiss, 1977, 1978, 1980). This chapter is divided into three parts that explore some of the reasons that this expectation is seldom met and suggest two consequences of the inability to conform to the rational model. The first part contains observations that emphasize the departures from rationality in information production. These are illustrated by examples from the behavior presented in Chapters 4 and 5. The second part explores how the lack of well-defined policy problems produces a need for bureaucratic analysts to provide interpretations of issues. The third part suggests that the undefined nature of policy problems influences the way that policy makers attend to the information bureaucratic analysts produce and that, consequently,

---

*For the purposes of this chapter I will use the term "rational" to refer to behavior described by the rational or bounded rational model. Using a less constrained definition of the term might produce the observation that it is not rational always to behave according to this model.

bureaucratic analysts "stockpile" interpretations for use when policy makers ask for them.

Departures from Rationality

Many people have commented that the work of bureaucratic analysts and other policy analysts does not contribute in a straightforward fashion to policy making. For the most part, however, they have looked at how the substance of analyses is not reflected in policy decisions. The following discussion goes beyond this by showing that even the process of producing information is inconsistent with the standards set by the rational or bounded rational models of policy making.

To be considered consistent with these standards the process must meet several basic criteria. First it should be intended for a specific decision. Second, there should be a well-specified problem, and the report being written should be relevant to and used in solving the problem. Third, the amount of time used to prepare the report should be bound by the emergence of a problem at one end and a decision at the other end. Fourth, the production of the report should be primarily oriented to influencing future outcomes of policy decisions.

What we observe is that the process of producing information often does not meet these expectations. First, many papers that bureaucratic analysts write are not intended for a specific decision process. Second, the immediate consequences and the decision relevance of the process are unknown and unpredictable. Third, the process takes an unpredictable but consequential amount of time. Fourth, the production of a report is primarily oriented to past actions and current context. Most of the examples that follow are taken from the detailed descriptions of the report writing process in Chapters 4 and 5, since most of the observations have to do with this process.

Intended Purpose of a Paper

The first observation is that most papers written by bureaucratic analysts are not driven by a specific decision process. Instead they are prompted by pre-established deadlines or by the bureaucratic analysts or contractors. The analysts whose activities are discussed in Chapter 5 were involved in writing twelve

TABLE 1

Relation of Papers to Decision Processes

Analyst	Paper	Related to Decision Process
Gregory	Methanol Report	No
Marvin	PPFG[a]	No[b]
Marvin	Methanol Report	No
Anne	PPFG[a]	No
Edna	Case Study Project	No
Edna	Statement of Problems Paper	No
Edna	Memorandum to General	Uncertain
Daniel	PPFG[a]	No
Daniel	Coal Policy Study	No
Daniel	Coal Competition Study	No
Daniel	Coal Leasing Goals	Uncertain
Daniel	Coal Production Goals	Yes

[a] Policy Planning and Fiscal Guidance Report.
[b] This PPFG paper was a revision of a paper related to a decision process.

papers over the three-month observation period.* Of these, only one was clearly tied to a specific decision process, one was a revision of a paper that had been written for a decision process before the observation period, and two had some possibility of becoming associated with decision processes. Thus, eight of the papers were not connected with decision processes at all. Table 1 contains the names of the analysts, descriptive titles of the papers, and their relation to a decision process.

If papers are not written for a decision process, then why are they written? Many reports are written because they are scheduled to be written. Some of these are scheduled regularly, such as annual reports. Many of the reports written during the observation period were of this sort. Daniel, Anne, and Marvin all wrote papers for the Policy Planning and Fiscal Guidance Report, an annual report produced by the policy office in which all of the issues that the policy office deals with are discussed. The four other papers that Daniel was involved in writing, commenting on, and concurring on were all required to be updated either annually or biennially.

Reports that are requested by Congress or the president also sometimes fall into the category of scheduled reports not as-

---

*One report, the methanol report, is counted twice since both Gregory and Marvin worked on it.

sociated with a decision process. These reports are requested through such vehicles as Congressional legislation or presidential speeches and often come with a deadline that is a year or more in the future. While those who request these reports may expect them to be used in future decisions,* the policy process is sufficiently unpredictable that such reports must be seen as essentially unrelated to any specific decision process. The NETS report described in Chapter 4 is an example of this. It was requested by President Carter in his First National Energy Plan of April 1977. It was completed in July 1980 and made public that September. Decisions were made about energy transportation before, during, and after its writing; the report had little connection to any of them.

Many other reports are written because policy analysts or contractors motivate the writing. Gregory was involved in a large project which he initiated, and Edna was trying to start such a project. Even small projects are initiated by the analysts. Marvin, for example, decided to embark upon revising some figures to be used in Gregory's report because he simply felt the methanol report would be better if these figures were more up-to-date.

Contractors also initiate report writing by submitting unsolicited proposals. These proposals suggest that the Department of Energy support the research the consultants think should be done. Marvin reviewed several such proposals.

Whether initiated by consultants, by policy analysts, or by the two working together, the work is not a response to a specific decision process. These reports may eventually become decision-relevant, and they are certainly justified as necessary for future decisions, but they are not undertaken for specific decision processes.

Relevance of the Process

The second observation is that in the short run the relevance of the process and its outcome are unknown and unpredictable.

---

*It has been argued that some of these reports are not intended for a decision process (Feldman and March, 1981). Using Edelman's terminology, their purpose may be symbolic reassurance rather than tangible change (Edelman, 1964, 1977).

Several illustrations support this, and they fall into two categories. One is that the immediate consequences of the process often seem obscure and unpredictable. The other is that the decision relevance of the process is uncertain.

The immediate consequences of the process often seem obscure and unpredictable in part because of the uncertainty involved in the process. There is uncertainty about whether the process will result in a paper, about whether the paper will have any influence, and ultimately about whether the effort makes sense. Considerable uncertainty was evident throughout the production of NETS. The January 1980 internal DOT option paper suggesting that NETS might be released as a DOT report rather than a joint DOE/DOT report and the desire by some in DOE to "trash" the report are indications of that uncertainty. While there was never any overall sense of how the NETS report would be used, even the potential usefulness seen by the participants interested in coal was made quite a bit less certain by the news that a separate report, "Moving U.S. Coal to Export Markets," had been taken to the energy summit meeting with President Carter.

In the railroad revenue case, comments were not agreed upon until a few hours before the filing deadline. Earlier that same day, the office director in the policy office suggested that it was not very important to complete the comments at all. At no time during the period of developing comments did anyone express the belief that the DOE comments would be decisive in the final ICC ruling.

The most obvious source of uncertainty in the slurry pipeline case is that no one knew what the content of the testimony would be until 24 hours before it had to be delivered. The analysts in the Department of Energy prepared a briefing and talking points without knowing whether or not they would be used. Many versions of the memorandum were written without knowing which ones would be read by whom or when.

Not only is there considerable uncertainty throughout the process, but the consequence of the process is also uncertain. As discussed above, in many instances, the paper is not related to a specific decision. Even if the process is oriented to a specifiable decision, it is not clear what part the document will or does play.

The slurry process, for example, appears to be the most directly decision-relevant of the processes described in Chapter 4. Many players that were far more influential than the analysts were involved. The White House staff, for instance, was involved from the beginning. The Secretaries of Energy and Interior also argued their positions directly to the president. There is evidence that the arguments made by the analysts were attended to (see Chapter 8). There is also, however, evidence that the politics, predispositions, and power of the major players—President Reagan, Secretaries James Edwards and James Watt—determined the final decision.

The process engaged in to produce the railroad revenue adequacy comments was also related to a decision—what the final regulations should be. The ICC had, however, already engaged in an internal decision-making process that had resulted in the proposed rulemaking published in the Federal Register, complete with an explanation for why this proposal was considered most suitable. In addition, the DOE comments carried with them neither political clout nor outstanding expertise. Many organizations that were commenting (e.g., the railroads and the coal companies) had much more at stake in this issue than the DOE. They were able to devote resources commensurate with that importance to their activities. They hired, or already employed, people who had been experts for years in railroad accounting. They could have analyses available to them that were far beyond the reach of DOE's commenting group. While the DOE could have had the political clout if upper management had chosen to get involved, they did not. This was not lost on the DOE participants. In fact, one of the rationales for the need to file comments was that if the Department of Energy did not comment, it would have no claim to future legal standing on this issue. This may have been an implicit recognition of the decision irrelevance of this particular action.

Thus, the process of even those papers that are intended for specific decisions indicates great uncertainty about the reasons for engaging in the process. Contrary to the expectation that the paper will be relevant to and used in solving a well-specified problem, closer scrutiny of the process reveals considerable uncertainty about its completion, its relevance, and its impact.

The Problem of Time

The third observation is that the process takes time and the amount of time needed is unpredictable. It took more than three years from beginning to end for the NETS process. From the time the first draft arrived at DOE to the time DOE concurred on the report took more than three months. The slurry testimony started in the summer of 1981 and continued through November 16, 1981, again taking more than three months. The time taken for the railroad revenue report was quite a bit shorter than the other two; it was produced between January 6 and January 23, a little more than two weeks. While these are the actual production times for these reports, each of them made use of already existing reports and agreements. For this reason, all underestimate the amount of time it would take to write a report from scratch.

The three reports were time-consuming in another sense. All three required most of the staff participants' days for some amount of the time that they were being produced. For NETS this period was the couple of weeks while DOE and DOT were jointly rewriting the draft. For DOE staff the period just prior to that was also very full with NETS-related activities. For the slurry testimony this period occurred between October 16 and October 29 while the memorandum to the president was being rewritten. For railroad revenue the whole two-week period was characterized by intense activity on this one issue.

Not only does the process require a substantial investment of time, but also the amount of time to completion is uncertain. Deadlines are often imposed, but they are also extended or simply not met. When NETS was finally delivered, it was more than a year overdue. Several interim deadlines were not met. For instance, the initial May 5 deadline for DOE comments was not met; the June 10 goal for completing the revision was not met; and the July 25 deadline for formal concurrence was not met. Deadlines were also extended in the slurry pipeline and railroad revenue cases. Furthermore, deadlines are often not really deadlines. They are, instead, bureaucratic signals or maneuvers in the negotiating process.

Thus, the relation of the process to its time frame is considerably more fluid than expected. The expectation consistent with the problem-solving perspective is that the process would fit within the frame established by the emergence and the resolution of a problem. Instead what we find is that the time required is heavily influenced by such features of the process as what information is being requested and from whom, how much conflict there is among the offices on the concurrence list, and how much groundwork has been laid for this paper by previous papers. Thus, there is a partial reversal of the expectation: the process influences the time frame.

Relation to Context

The fourth observation is that the production of a report is influenced by features of the past and current contexts in which the report is written. These include earlier actions, past report-writing experiences, and pressures for consensus. People writing reports do not know if the reports will be used or how. They do not know which aspects of which issues will become controversial and which ones will cease to be questioned. They are able, however, to figure out what needs to be done to produce a report that everyone can approve.

The report-writing process unfolds as different participants do what seems to them to be the appropriate next step. The process is pushed as much from what came before (the previous action) as from what comes next. Paper writing is essentially responsive. At the most general level, the processes described in Chapter 4 were responses to drafts of papers seen as unacceptable. Actions within the process, however, were also the result of preceding actions or situations. The following are a few examples. In NETS, the joint DOE/DOT rewriting came about because of the overwhelming negative reaction to the draft report. Breaking up into small groups to deal with the coal chapter was a reaction to the large number of people interested in different aspects of the chapter. In the slurry pipeline case, the deadline for commenting on the memorandum to the president was moved because the Department of Energy participants claimed that they had not had enough time to respond and had major disagreements with the material in the memorandum. In the railroad revenue case, the participants responded to one another's efforts to gain control of the process and to determine the contents of the paper.

Previous report-writing processes that dealt with the same issue or involved the same people influence the present process. While it is, of course, impossible to say what the process would have been like if any factors had been different, we can speculate on what features of the situation seem to have had a significant influence. Part of the NETS context was that the financial condition of the railroads was an issue that had received joint DOE/DOT attention as a completely separate matter in the past. During the report writing, this was one of the most problematic issues and the only one on which the Secretary's office had to intervene.

In the slurry scenario, the department had many times taken the position favoring granting federal eminent domain for coal slurry pipelines. While the same people were not always involved, every time people gathered to discuss this issue there had mostly been consensus among them. During the process outlined in Chapter 4, Department of Energy responses to memoranda were generated without having to have an internal DOE process over what the response should be. Similarly, though it was not clear whether the head of the program office or the head of the policy office would give the testimony for the Department of Energy, it did not matter which office's staff members wrote the testimony because of the consistent agreement and close working relations among offices on this issue.

In the railroad revenue case, the context was one of conflict. Previous filings with the same organizational participants (though not necessarily the same people) had produced a history of discord. In addition, a commenting process involving the same people had just been completed. It had also been marked by conflict. The process summarized in Chapter 4 certainly lived up to the expectation of conflict and discord.

Pressures for consensus also influence the process of report writing. Top managers expect that agreement will be reached at the staff level. Pressure may be exerted by superiors or other higher-level management to encourage agreement. Several instances of pressure from superiors to encourage staff agreement were evident during the NETS process. The person from the Secretary's office in DOE who sat in on the first joint meeting, the May 19 memo from the head of Resource Applications, and the intervention from the Secretary's office when the Economic Regulatory Administration did not produce the wording for the section on the financial condition of the railroads are the most prominent. This pressure was not present in the slurry case. It was, however, expressed most explicitly in the railroad revenue case where the General Counsel staff member's superior refused to become involved at the same time that the policy office staff member's superior said that if the people working on the comments could not agree, then the department should not file anything.

These observations illustrate the effects of the context on the process. While requests for information are certainly part of the context, they are only that. The possible future impact of the paper tends to be displaced as an influence on the process by more immediate and more tangible influences. These include the relations of the participants to one another, their histories of dealing with the issue and with one another, and the pressures of superiors to come to agreement. While these features are generally relevant, each process has a different context and, thus, different features that influence its development.

Conclusion

These observations are quite different from those derived from the problem-solving perspective. This may make report writing seem ineffectual or senseless. However, the problem-solving perspective is an inappropriate standard for the work that bureaucratic analysts do, because the context does not fit the assumptions implicit in the perspective. One important assumption is that there are well-specified problems. Where this is not true, a process of interpretation is necessary for proposing possible ways to think about the issue. In addition, since problems are not well specified, policy makers cannot request information far enough in advance for the bureaucratic analysts to provide it. This, in effect, produces a need for papers to be written before they are requested.

The Need for Interpretation

The world of policy making is not nearly so straightforward as suggested by the simple problem-solving vision (Lynn, 1978). Policy problems are not necessarily well defined (Rich, 1981a; Weiss, 1978). Policy makers are confronted with a never-ending jumble of ambiguous issues rather than a neat sequence of problems (Cohen, March, and Olsen, 1972; Lynn, 1978; March and Olsen, 1976). It is often not even clear whether an issue is a problem or a solution.

Defining Policy Problems

Most issues can be defined as either problems or solutions, or as both. Space flight, for instance, is an issue. For some people it is a problem that requires vast material and technological resources. For others it is a solution to the technological and military competition between the United States and the Soviet Union. Battleships are an issue. Some people want to define them as problems for which mothballing and dismantling are solutions. Others promote them as solutions for problems such as the Falkland incident. Educational testing is an issue. For some it is a problem defined by discrimination and poor predictive powers. For others it is a solution (or at least a partial solution) to the problem of choosing from a pool of applicants about whom very little information is available.

Even this description is overly simple. Issues are generally not just problems or solutions. Educational testing, for example, can be altered so that it is less biased, or it can be supplemented by other predictors of future success. Similarly, it can be used not only to make choices, but also to improve our understanding of skills that are valued and the ways in which schools and teachers are more or less successful in teaching them. Indeed, this understanding can help people evaluate whether or not the skills these tests select for are appropriate measures of success.

The different ways of looking at an issue that lead to thinking about them as problems or solutions may be called "faces" (Allison, 1971; Halperin, 1974). Any issue may have several such faces. The face you see of an issue determines whether it appears to be a problem or solution, as well as the properties of the problems and the appropriateness of different solutions. Students of bureaucratic politics have suggested that the face individuals or organizations see or promote is determined by their interests. They claim that individuals and organizations attempt to define an issue in accordance with their interests and that they use their power to construct definitions of issues consistent with the social reality they favor (Pfeffer, 1977).

Giving meaning to an issue is, however, not simple. While both power and interests are important, neither is straightforward. Power is constrained. Definitions of policy issues are not dictated by powerful legislators, presidents, or interest groups. Instead perspectives are shared, influence one another, and shift over time. They are constrained by cultural values and shared assumptions (Dahl, 1961; Lindblom, 1965).

Similarly, interests are certainly no more a given than are problems or solutions. Even the mandate of an organization only constrains, but does not determine, its interests. The Department of Energy may, by definition and mandate, have an interest in the development of energy resources. That, in itself, does not tell us very much about the actions or perspectives the department is likely to take. For instance, windmills and nuclear reactors are both sources of energy. The interests specified by officials of the department will determine the likelihood of action in these two areas of energy development.

The production of information that bureaucratic analysts engage in is an opportunity for organizations to define and develop their interests in an issue. In this process past interests are reinterpreted, and new interests are discovered. The understandings derived from these interests are shared and influence one another. Thus, the report-writing process is fundamentally a process of interpretation.

Interpretation

Interpretation involves categorization. We understand an issue by relating characteristics to it. Students of phenomenology have demonstrated the effect of language and categorization on the ways that we understand the world (Bateson, 1972; Blumer, 1969; Goffman, 1974, 1983; Schutz, 1970; Schutz and Luckmann,

1973). One of the primary effects of categorization is its ability to draw our attention to some features of a situation and away from others. Bateson and Goffman have both used the notion of "frame" to discuss this phenomenon. A conceptual or psychological frame delineates what is relevant from what is irrelevant; it designates what is the appropriate context within which to understand a given phenomenon (Bateson, 1972; Goffman, 1974).

Thus, when we associate discrimination with educational testing, we make equality a relevant concern. When we associate it with making admissions decisions, we make pragmatism relevant. When we associate energy development with military might, we make technological development more relevant than if we associate energy development with income redistribution.

This process of associating concerns with issues affects what kind of problems we think we have and also what kinds of solutions seem appropriate to them. Edelman (1977) claims that the ways in which we categorize or attach language to problems has a strong effect on the kinds of solutions considered appropriate for them. "From subtle linguistic evocations and associated governmental actions we get a great many of our beliefs about what our problems are, their causes, their seriousness, our success or failure in coping with them, which aspects are fixed and which are changeable, and what impacts they have upon which groups of people. We are similarly cued into beliefs about which authorities can deal with which problems, the levels of merit and competence of various groups of the population, the benchmarks for judging public policies, and who are allies and who are enemies" (Edelman, 1977, p. 41).

Written documents play an important role in this interpretive process. In the process of writing, an author must take a complex reality and structure it into a linear, more simple representation (Cicourel, 1968). Because of the need to make sense within a reasonable time and space limitation, only details relevant to the proposed interpretation can be presented. Details that may support other interpretations are omitted. The written document establishes a frame that becomes part of an organizational memory. In the future, when the issue, event, person, or situation is reconsidered, this information will be influential because it reminds people to pay attention to certain features and because it provides a basis for comparison. Thus, the structuring that occurs affects how future as well as current readers understand the subject of the written document.

Bureaucratic analysts write papers in which they make connections between certain facts and concerns and a policy issue. They create a structure or frame for thinking about the issue. This structure helps to define the problematic features of the issue and the outline of an appropriate solution. It is influenced by the interests that the analysts involved in writing the paper represent. (As we saw in Chapter 4, these interests can be attached to a number of different features of the paper. Substantive interests are, however, the most pervasive and the simplest to use as illustrations.) Analysts from the policy office will, for instance, be concerned with the consistency of the report with general policies of the department; analysts from the General Counsel's office will be concerned with the legality of what is in the report and the consistency with current legal actions the department is involved in. Representatives from offices dealing with the production of statistical information will be concerned about the proper use of this information. Analysts from offices dealing with environmental or economic impacts will make sure that facts and concerns relevant to these interests are included in the paper.

The interpretation of an issue contained in a paper is determined by the inclusion and exclusion of information. The information contained in the paper is largely a function of two things: first, what information has been considered relevant in the past and has been included in past papers; second, what interests are represented by analysts writing the current paper and what agreements they are able to make when their interests conflict. This process of interpretation is explored in greater detail in the next chapter. It is an essential part of what bureaucratic analysts do and how they contribute to the policy-making process.

The Need for Inventories

The fact that policy problems are not well defined has another effect on the production of information. This effect occurs because policy makers often have a hard time knowing what items will be on the agenda and what specific form they will take

(Kingdon, 1984; Lynn, 1978). As a result, they cannot specify what information they need (Rich, 1981; Weiss, 1978). By the time they are able to specify what information they need, it may be so close to the time when a decision will be made that there is not enough time to engage in the time-consuming process required to produce good information.

Bureaucratic analysts work in a situation characterized most of the time by a lack of attention by decision makers or policy makers. Many reports they write are not read; many contracts they set up are not used; much expertise they acquire is not called upon. Decisions about policies seem to be made on the basis of politics and personal loyalties rather than the information and expertise that the analysts have to offer. Observers have recognized this (Kraft, 1981; Rosenbaum, 1981; Stever, 1980; Wildavsky and Tenenbaum, 1981); policy makers recognize it (Okrent, 1981); and bureaucratic analysts recognize it (field notes 5/1/80, 5/6/80, 5/22/80; interviews 10 and 28).

Though usually inattentive, policy makers are not always so. In fact, from time to time decision makers will call on the policy staff to help inform a decision they are making. While the policy staff are aware that this will sometimes happen, and individual staff members may have theories about what issues and at what stages their help will be requested, surprises often occur. The issues are sometimes important, sometimes unimportant. They are sometimes marked by a great deal of conflict, sometimes quite uncontroversial.

Thus, the context in which bureaucratic analysts work is one in which attention from policy makers is generally absent and in which it is not clear when or for what issues policy makers will call upon the staff. Furthermore, attention from policy makers will be brief when it occurs at all, and the staff must be ready to respond to it quickly. In other words, policy staff know that there will be demands for their work, but they don't know what will be requested or when, only that they will have to respond quickly once a request for information is made.

Consequently, the amount of time available once policy makers ask for information bureaucratic analysts can provide is substantially less than it takes to produce the information. This context makes the problem-solving perspective an inappropriate way to view this behavior. If papers were written only when it was clear they would be used for problem solving, then the information would not be available for use by the time the policy makers wanted it.

This way of thinking about providing information may seem confusing at first. An analogy with libraries may help. Imagine if a library ordered books only when they were requested by a patron. It may take weeks or even months before the book is received and ready to circulate. In the meantime, the patron may very well have resolved the need for the book or lost interest in it. This procedure may reduce the number of unused library books; it would certainly reduce the usefulness of the library.

In policy making, the report-writing process is analogous to the ordering of a book from a publisher; and the policy maker, to the patron. (To make this analogy even stronger, imagine that libraries ask authors to write books only after information is requested by a patron.) Because of the nature of report writing and the agreement or concurrence process, adequate preparation of information often takes longer than is available when a policy maker asks for it. Since it is important that the demands for information be met, it makes sense to prepare for them in advance.

We can think of bureaucratic analysts as preparing and stockpiling information for future, as yet unspecified, policy-making situations. This information can be made readily available when policy makers ask for it. Policy makers may be able to use an already existing and agreed-upon report, or analysts may update a report in which many of the time-consuming conflicts have already been resolved. Thus, the work of bureaucratic analysts may be thought of as developing and maintaining an inventory of policy positions and reports that policy makers may request when needed.

In other words, bureaucratic analysts prepare for future demands at least as much as they respond to current ones. This is not an unusual occurrence. Libraries, again, provide a good analogy. They have stacks filled to satisfy the reading preferences of the unknown future user. The specific books or other publications that will be requested by users is seldom known by those responsible for making new acquisitions. Though it may take several weeks or months to complete the process of choosing, ordering, receiving, and cataloging new publications, users will expect the time between making their requests and having them fulfilled to be substantially shorter than that. To deal with this context, libraries maintain inventories of publications. Some of these will never be used, others will be, but no one can predict when or how often. Peacetime military forces perform a similar function. They develop repertoires of capabilities in preparation for future wars with unknown properties to be fought in unknown places.

The four observations made about report writing are consistent with the notion of an inventory. The first was that papers are not intended for a specific decision process, and the second was that in the short run the process and its outcome are irrelevant. Inventories need not be relevant to what is occurring at the time the inventory is being developed since they are preparation for future contingencies. The third observation was that the process takes time and the amount of time needed is unpredictable. Maintaining an inventory pays off when the time it takes to make an item available is less than the time between request and due date. Even when the process takes a relatively short time, the uncertainty about the length of the process makes "postrequest" production a risky strategy.

The fourth observation was that the production of a report is primarily oriented to past actions and current context. The process takes on the appearance of a routine, not in the sense that the same thing is produced or in the same manner, but in the sense that a pattern of behavior exists that helps people figure out what needs to be done next given what has already happened. People may be working on very different types of papers under very different circumstances, yet they are guided by the general knowledge of how to write a report, how to push it through the concurrence process, and so forth. In the absence of a larger goal, the goal of completing this task at hand becomes the focus of attention (Gregory, 1982; Howton, 1969). In this case, completing the task is defined by producing a document of a certain form that is agreed to by a specified set of people.

Conclusion

In this chapter we have seen how the context of policy making influences the production of information. The uncertainty and unpredictability of the context make it nearly impossible for the production of information to conform to the expectations promoted by the problem-solving perspective.

Report writing constitutes an indirect contribution to decision making rather than a direct one. Part of this indirect contribution involves the production of an inventory of positions and papers about policy areas. This inventory may be called upon at any time to supply policy makers with information relevant to an issue that has become active. The resulting stockpile of information is not, however, the only contribution.

The contents of the inventory are interpretations of issue. Bureaucratic analysts develop these interpretations, or ways of understanding issues, as they represent their organization's interests and interact with other analysts representing other interests. The next chapter explores further the nature of these interpretations and the role bureaucratic analysts have in producing them.

CHAPTER 8

Properties of the Inventory

THE LAST CHAPTER suggested that in producing reports bureaucratic analysts create inventories of issue interpretations. This chapter examines the nature of these interpretations. It illustrates how bureaucratic analysts influence their substance both indirectly and directly. It explains why interpretations produced by bureaucratic analysts are unique in the type of information they provide. Finally, the use of the inventories of interpretations is discussed.

Influencing Interpretations

Bureaucratic analysts influence the interpretations contained in reports through their participation in paper writing and through the other tasks they perform as part of their responsibilities. When they write reports, they directly negotiate the substance of the interpretation. When they perform other tasks their effect on interpretations is indirect.

Bureaucratic analysts spend much of their time producing written reports that contain information about policy issues. As discussed in the previous chapter, the process they engage in is, essentially, one of framing policy issues. They make connections between specific facts and concerns and the issue. They include the facts and concerns that they consider to be relevant to understanding the issue and exclude others.

The analysts do not make decisions about what facts and concerns are relevant capriciously or in isolation. They are constrained by the interests of the organization they work for and the position this organization has taken in the past on the issue.

They are also constrained by the fact that they nearly always have to have agreement on the substance of the paper from many other organizations.

A completed report is a set of statements that all of the concurring organizations can support or "sign off" on. These statements may be supported by everyone because they avoid controversial issues, or they may reflect the hard work of resolving conflicts. There is often disagreement among the organizations on the concurrence list about both factual and analytical information included in the report. For most papers there is some mix of resolvable and unresolvable disagreements. Finding a set of statements that all the signing organizations will agree to is a process in which bureaucratic analysts often participate.

There are many examples of this in the three reports described in Chapter 4. In each case, the analysts argued about which facts and concerns would be associated with the issue in the paper and which ones would be omitted. In the NETS report the disputes were between the Department of Transportation and the Department of Energy. In the slurry case they were between the Department of Interior and the Department of Energy. In the railroad revenue adequacy case they were between the Economic Regulatory Administration on the one hand and the General Counsel's Office and the policy office of the Department of Energy on the other.

In the slurry case, for example, the Department of Energy wanted to include in the memorandum to the president information about the precedents for granting eminent domain for energy transportation. This included information about when and why eminent domain had been granted for natural gas lines and electric wires. This information would help to make the argument that granting eminent domain would be appropriate for coal slurry pipelines. The Department of Interior did not favor granting eminent domain to coal slurry pipelines. Therefore, they argued that this information was not relevant to the current issue. Similarly, the Department of Energy sought to include information that argued that slurry pipelines would have little effect on railroad coal traffic while the Department of Interior sought to include information to the contrary.

Bureaucratic analysts also influence interpretations contained in papers through less direct means. In Chapter 5 I showed that as part of doing a good job, bureaucratic analysts must confront the problems of obtaining information necessary for performing tasks, gaining support and approval for their work, and establishing their role among other people who deal with the same issue. Their efforts affect who participates in writing papers, what information is available for inclusion in papers, and what information is actually contained in a particular paper. Through these means their activities influence the interpretations of policy issues.

Negotiating Interpretations

The interpretations bureaucratic analysts produce are essentially negotiated agreements. While they contain information from many sources, they are not simply compilations of this information. As discussed in Chapter 7, the decisions about what information to include and what to exclude are made, in part, on the basis of what interests are represented by those writing the report. This is not to suggest that reports are biased in the pejorative sense of the word. The analysts are not seeking to give a false impression or understanding. It is simply true that all reports are biased in that choices always have to be made about what information is relevant and should be included.

Relevance is related to organizational interests. A person from the Department of Energy concerned with energy development and a person from the Interstate Commerce Commission concerned with regulation or deregulation of transportation will, for instance, differ about what information is relevant to an issue concerning energy transportation. Neither is wrong or right. They simply see the issue from different vantage points. In the process of writing a paper analysts from these two organizations have to negotiate about what information both can agree is relevant and appropriate.

The process of negotiating agreements has an adversarial quality to it. Representatives of the organizations involved act as advocates of their organization's interests. Each organization gathers information about and develops positions concerning its interests. Each organization is responsible for making sure that its interests are represented in positions that are taken by the department or the government as a whole (Kaufman, 1981). The Economic Regulatory Administration's strong position on the financial condition of the railroads and the Department of Energy's support for eminent domain for coal slurry pipelines are two illustrations of this advocacy.

Concurrence Lists

The concurrence process is one of the mechanisms through which organizations protect their interests. Whenever a paper is written, it must be signed by many different organizations. The specific organizations vary with the paper. They may include several cabinet-level departments or may consist entirely of offices within one department or agency.* When the heads of these organizations sign a report, they are signifying that they concur with and support what the report says.

Ideally, a concurrence list includes the organizations that are advocates for all the interests that might be affected by the issue under consideration. What organizations are included is influenced by who is making up the list and the knowledge they have about who has interests in the topic the paper is about. Organizations that were on the last concurrence list for a given topic are likely to be on the next list as well. (The process is, of course, also subject to the normal pressures of politics and limited cognition.)

Determining which organizations are relevant to a given issue or request for information is not only a question of history, politics, and knowledge, but also of interpretation or perspective. The perspective from which one sees an issue influences which organizations appear to be related to the issue. The description of the National Energy Transportation Study (NETS) provides a good example of this. For the most part, interdepartmental reports on coal transportation included the representatives from the Departments of Energy and Transportation that participated in the NETS report. Sometimes more people were included depending on the topics covered. However, towards the end of writing NETS, another report on coal transportation emerged

---

*For simplicity I will refer from here on to both whole organizations and subunits of an organization such as an office or a division simply as organizations.

that none of the people working on NETS had known about. How could all of these organizations with interests in coal transportation be left off the concurrence list for a report on this topic? It is, of course, possible that the omissions were deliberate and conspiratorial. An easier explanation exists, however. The report "Moving U.S. Coal to Export Markets" was originated by an organization concerned with *international* rather than domestic transportation of coal. As the title implies the study dealt with domestic transportation only as it relates to the export of coal. The people who they generally work with are those who deal with international issues. In the Department of Energy, this was the assistant secretary of International Affairs rather than the parts of the department involved in writing reports on domestic coal transportation. Thus, two reports covering nearly identical ground were read, commented on, and approved by two nonoverlapping groups of people.

Negotiating Process

Representatives from the offices on the concurrence list are usually involved in the production of the relevant document. These people promote and protect the interests represented by their offices. The content of the interpretation depends on what interests are represented. In NETS and the railroad revenue adequacy filing, for instance, representatives from the Economic Regulatory Administration made sure that the interpretations included information about how, by taking advantage of shippers who had to use them, the railroads could subsidize the shipping of other products and so increase their overall market. If the head of the Economic Regulatory Administration had not had to concur on these papers, the representatives from this office would not have helped to write the report, and this feature of the interpretation would not have been included.

This example is particularly clear because only the representatives from the Economic Regulatory Administration wanted this perspective included in these reports. Some others opposed it; some were neutral. The perspective was included because it was considered absolutely central by the people representing the Economic Regulatory Administration. Though organizational representatives generally do have preferences about what to include or exclude, not all parts of an interpretation are so clearly attributable to one organization or its representatives.

Bureaucratically Produced Interpretations

It is the representation of interests and the need for agreement that makes the papers of bureaucratic analysts especially relevant to issue interpretation. Other analysts produce ways of thinking about issues, too (Wildavsky, 1979). Certainly when academics write policy analyses, they are proposing a way of viewing an issue. These ideas are important and useful. However, since they are not produced under the same conditions as those of the bureaucratic analysts, they do not contain the same information, nor do they have the same effect.

If properly constituted, this bureaucratic process can provide policy makers with information that is otherwise unavailable to them. It brings together disparate and often conflicting interests and encourages them to find as much agreement as possible. The incentives to find agreement coupled with the incentives to protect interests creates a unique situation that, in turn, provides two kinds of information. One is information about where agreements are more or less possible among the disparate and conflicting interests represented by the organizations participating in the bureaucratic process. This information should give a reasonable (though not perfect) sense of where possible agreements lie among the interests in the society in general. The second kind of information is about where in the bureaucracy there are shared understandings and where there are conflicts over the issue. This is particularly important when, as is common, the bureaucracy is involved in implementing the policy (Brunsson, 1985; Pressman and Wildavsky, 1973).

The process does not, of course, unfailingly provide this information. If concurrence lists are not carefully composed or if relevant interests are not represented in the bureaucracy, the information will not fulfill its potential. Likewise, if parts of an organization critical to implementation are not included in the interpretation-building process, they may not share the same perspective as represented in the papers. Imbalances in the concurrence list or in the negotiating process could result in misleading information. Recognizing the special properties of this information, however, may increase both the appreciation of it by policy makers and the attention given to its proper production by officials in the bureaucracy.

The Use of Interpretations

The production of this unique information is not the only effect of this bureaucratic process, for the process has a diffuse influence on the way an issue is understood. The bureaucracy is only one of many factors that influence how an issue is understood by policy makers, members of the bureaucracy, and the public. Other factors include natural events, acts of the legislature, presidents, and the Supreme Court, the media, and academia (Derthick and Quirk, 1985; Fritschler, 1983; Muir, 1973). Academia plays a role similar to the one ascribed to the bureaucracy though through a different process. Both encourage individuals and groups of people to look at issues from varying perspectives, to promote ideas consistent with these perspectives, and to share these ideas in a manner that allows them to be scrutinized and modified as well as adopted or rejected.

These processes have a diffuse effect on the way an issue is understood. Accounts of the development of understandings, most commonly associated with scientific fields, describe the circuitous and often time-consuming manner in which new understandings about phenomena emerge (Dyson, 1979; Kuhn, 1970; Rudwick, 1985; Watson, 1968). Tracing the path of new understandings of social and policy issues may be more difficult because the influences are more diverse and the networks less distinct. However, there is no reason to believe that the fundamental process is different. Indeed, Derthick and Quirk (1985) have argued that such a process was instrumental in bringing about deregulation in the late 1970's and early 1980's. Rein (1976) has made a similar argument about the development of welfare policy and health care. Goodwin's (1981) edited volume on the development of energy policy also recounts a number of examples of the emergence of ideas, most notably the idea of a department of energy.

These changes in policy decisions are only the most visible influence of the interpretations. It almost always takes years from the first emergence of an interpretation to the occurrence of visible change in policy. Derthick and Quirk, for example, describe how regulatory reform occurred only after the analytical principles had been thoroughly accepted by academic economists for some time. Even then, change depended on serendipitous events and people who were positioned and ready to take advantage of them. The process from emergence to acceptance of an idea has been likened to the body's acceptance of a new organ: "New ideas, like new organs, may first be rejected by the body, but then gradually experience semi-acceptance, until finally the organ is incorporated" (Rein, 1976, p. 119).

The contribution of bureaucratic analysts to this slow process is fundamental: analysts produce ideas about how to think about issues. These ideas are not necessarily accepted by the policy-making community, however. Instead, they bounce around from one report to another. They move over time and from one set of organizational interests to another. Later report writers confront the ideas of earlier report writers (Rich, 1982). Report writers in one part of the bureaucracy confront the ideas of report writers in other parts. In this way the ideas are scrutinized by many people with different perspectives.

As the idea moves from one setting to another, it may continue to look like a good idea. It may look like a good idea to some and a bad idea to others. It may be decidedly rejected. Opinions may vary either because of the different interests of the reviewers or because of their different knowledge or both. The process does not necessarily alter the quality of result, even though it is, in part, responsible for the result.

An idea may bounce around for years before it is implemented—and, of course, many ideas are never implemented. Some gain very wide popularity and change the way that people think about the issues (e.g., providing nonsmoking areas in public places). Others circulate until they reach decision makers who are ready for them and settings in which they can be reasonably implemented (e.g., desegregation of schools and the U.S. Supreme Court).

Given this slow and gradual character of the process of influencing understandings one would not expect to be able to trace many effects on policy making over a short observation period. There was one instance, described in Chapter 4, in which a concern about the slurry pipeline issue promoted by the Department of Energy analysts was picked up directly in a memorandum from the president to the Secretary of Interior and used in testimony before Congress. Such instances happen rarely, however. Bureaucratic analysts may only be able to see the effects of their efforts after many years of promoting an interpretation.

Conclusion

The process whereby information comes to be used by policy makers is complicated rather than straightforward (Hofferbert, 1974; Lindblom, 1968). No one completely controls it. Most people have little control at all. Yet actions can have an effect. The process depends on the development and dissemination of a steady stream of ideas.

Bureaucratic analysts are one source of this stream (they are also in the stream). Their activities affect the definition of problems and the composition of participants in the problem-solving process (Weiss, 1980). As they produce information about an issue, they engage in acts that help to shape future policy-making settings. For this reason, their work is very important even though it is seldom directly used in the decision for which it was produced.

CHAPTER 9

Problem Solving Versus Interpretation:

From the Bureaucratic Analysts' Perspective

WHILE MANY ANALYSTS recognize that they do not often, or ever, make direct contributions to policy making, with few exceptions they tend to think that they *should*. Many of them are cynical about this situation. They tell stories about times when it looked like their analyses were going to have an influence, but then the president or a key legislator decided on a political basis and ignored the information. They laugh at new upper-level officials who are excited about the potential impact of studies that the analysts have done several times before without seeing any effect on policies.

This chapter suggests that analysts have a hard time valuing the work they do because they are captive to the problem-solving or rational perspective discussed in previous chapters. Two effects of this perspective on the way analysts view their work are explored. One effect is that analysts have a narrow definition for the use of information, which tends to make it difficult for them to see the importance of what they do. The second effect is that they see the routines through which they produce information as obstructing their work rather than as producing a unique kind of information. In short, the problem-solving perspective held by bureaucratic analysts keeps them from appreciating much of the work they do.

The Problem-Solving Perspective

The analysts encountered in doing this study were, for the most part, smart and insightful. They spent time thinking about their roles as analysts and what role their offices or departments had in policy making. They did not mindlessly adopt the problem-solving perspective. It is, however, hard to avoid, for a number of reasons. First of all, it has broad legitimacy in our society (Feldman and March, 1981; Lindblom, 1965; Wildavsky, 1979); even authors who criticize the positivist framework of policy analysis often attempt to retain an essentially rationalistic perspective (Bozeman, 1986). This legitimacy is reinforced in much of the training that analysts receive at universities and professional schools. Many analytical methods such as cost-benefit analysis or program evaluation assume a rational perspective. Thus, when the analysts arrive at the work place, the perspective is already well established.

In the work place, analysts are surrounded by other people who believe that the proper use for their work is in providing solutions for policy problems. This value is reinforced by peers and superiors who get excited about the possibility of contributing directly to policy making and by rewards that come to the analysts when they happen to make such contributions. These rewards often include attention from high-level officials, superiors, and peers, recognition awards, and offers of better and more interesting jobs, as well as the intrinsic reward of having an influence on policy. Though opportunities to contribute directly may not happen often, their effect can be very strong.* Even analysts who have never had such an opportunity can be assured of such possibilities when they see or hear of it happening to another analyst. In these ways, the bureaucratic setting encourages belief in a problem-solving perspective even when there is not much evidence to sustain it.

The belief that what they are or should be doing is problem solving makes it difficult for analysts to adopt or value an inter-

---

*The strength of the effect may be partly due to the intermittent nature of the reinforcement. Psychologists have found that intermittent reinforcement produces the most enduring effects (Berger and Lambert, 1968).

pretive perspective of their work, for two reasons. One is that
the two perspectives have very different definitions of the use of
information. The other is that the two perspectives value very
differently the way work is done.

Standards for Information Use

The Problem-Solving Perspective

The problem-solving perspective is an extension of means-
end rationality. According to this notion, a decision is prompted
by a problem. Problems stimulate the search for solutions. Problems always precede solutions. Decision making is the process
of generating solutions and selecting among them in order to resolve a problem (Allison, 1971; Downs, 1957; Luce and Raiffa,
1957). Information is important in this process as a means of
choosing among alternative solutions.

The standard for information use implied by this perspective
is *direct* use in policy making. This means that the reports con-
taining the information are attended to by people involved in
making the decisions and that the information influences the
policy outcome. This standard implies that each instance of policy making is a discrete event and that for each of these events
there is a well-defined problem and possible solutions. If a policy paper is not read by policy makers or the people who advise
them and if it has no discernible impact on the policy decision
under current consideration, then, according to this definition,
the information has not been used.

The Interpretive Perspective

The interpretive perspective places less emphasis than the
problem-solving perspective on conclusions. The goal of interpretation is not necessarily action. The standard for evaluation
is understanding rather than action (Goodman, 1978) or even explanation (Healy, 1986). Instead, policy making consists of continuous efforts to gain better understandings both of the world
in which we must occasionally act and of the values we hold that
are relevant to action. When we do act, the way we currently

understand the world influences what actions we think are appropriate or even possible.

When bureaucratic analysts produce interpretations of issues, they are contributing to the information that is available to help policy makers and the public understand issues. They also contribute directly to the understandings of the people who read the paper in which an interpretation is contained. The information gained may be about the issue per se or may be about the relation between a specific interest and that issue. The person receiving the information may ignore it, refute it, adopt it, or some combination of these. Thus, the influence any paper has may inhibit, promote, or have no effect or some combination of these on the interpretation it contains.

The image that most closely portrays this effect is one of throwing pebbles into a turbulent pool of water. Ripples radiate from the places the pebbles enter the water. Some ripples go in one direction; some in the opposite direction. Some of these ripples are overwhelmed by the turbulence of the water. The effect may be very difficult to observe. It may not be the effect desired by the person throwing the pebbles. It may be negligible compared to either the existing turbulence or other shocks that the pool receives. It may take years of throwing pebbles before an effect is noticeable.

This perspective offers little hope for bureaucratic analysts to have an impact on policy making in a short period of time. If it happens, it is serendipitous, the result of being at the right place at the right time. The standard for information use from this perspective is indirect, uncontrolled, and long-term. If you view the world from a problem-solving perspective, it may be difficult to value or even to see the nature of the contribution to policy making that the interpretive perspective suggests. Bureaucratic analysts who view their work from the problem-solving perspective may not stay in their jobs long enough to see the impact that they have.

Standards for the Work Process

When asked about the length of time allowed for completion of assignments, one analyst responded, "There's never enough

time to do it right, but always enough time to do it over" (interview 27). This analyst was making a common complaint about
the conflict between the demands of the work process and the
desire to take enough time to do something "right." Routines
that govern the work process require that written reports be circulated fairly quickly for review. Established deadlines often
force circulation of reports when the authors feel there is still
much to do before the report is complete. The reviewers make
comments about the report. The authors then revise the report
in response to these comments. Thus, even though there is an
initial rush to produce the report, that is not the end of the process, but only a first step. There are nearly always revisions to be
made and time enough to make those changes.

The problem-solving perspective suggests that when bureaucratic analysts write a paper, they are providing information
relevant to solving a specific problem. Given this context, it
would be reasonable for the process of producing information to
be tailored to the current problem being solved and for the process to have as its goal the production of a solution. Having to
follow procedures that are similar from one paper-writing situation to another may appear to get in the way of performing the
task at hand. The procedures themselves may make it more difficult to produce a solution.

The routines that organize the bureaucratic analysts' work do
often appear to them to obstruct their ability to provide policy
makers with solutions. One reason for this is that routines are
not tailored to specific instances. A routine, by its nature, is
more appropriate for dealing with cases in general than it is for
dealing with any specific cases (Weber, 1946). Thus, while the
pattern of behavior may be a generally useful one, it may appear
to obstruct progress in any specific case.

Another reason that routines appear to obstruct work is that
they tend to emphasize process over outcome. What a routine
does for an organization is stabilize and regularize the work process. The use of impersonal rules, categorization of cases, delegation of authority, and centralization are all standard organizational routines that are aimed at producing stability (Crozier,
1964; Gouldner, 1954; Merton, 1936; Selznick, 1949). Using these
routines to gain control over the work process has some unantici-

pated consequences. Emphasis on uniformity and impersonality in decision making encourages bureaucrats to place more importance on the process of work than on the accomplishments. Following the rules and employing impersonal categories becomes more important than doing the work these routines were established to regularize. Bureaucrats are often accused, for example, of being more concerned that the paperwork for a case be in order than that the actions for which the paperwork is being filed be completed. Similarly, delegation of authority often leads to strict adherence to hierarchical chains of command. The military provides many examples of this adherence preventing important information from reaching the appropriate people (Wilensky, 1967; Wohlstetter, 1962). In short, routines codify a process. This often produces a situation in which the process becomes the end rather than the means (Howton, 1969).

The result is a host of bureaucratic pathologies. Rigidity, a failure to learn or adapt, and an inability adequately to perform a desired function are commonly noted (March and Simon, 1958). Crozier even goes so far as to define bureaucratic organizations in terms of this characteristic, observing that "a bureaucratic organization is an organization that cannot correct its behavior by learning from its errors" (1964, p. 187). Routines seem to obstruct what is essential to the performance of work.

This problem is particularly difficult to remedy in cases where there is no way to evaluate results. This happens in two instances: when the goal is unknown or unmeasurable and when the goals are known, but the means to them are not.

Where it is impossible to measure success, process takes the place of goals in evaluating the appropriateness of behavior. Judicial proceedings provide a good example of this. Success in achieving justice cannot be measured by how many convictions or acquittals there are or by how many cases are tried. In any single case, it is impossible to know what is the correct determination. The standard for evaluation is, therefore, stated in terms of proper process rather than desired outcomes. We establish the appropriateness of these proceedings by such measures as whether the parties have proper counsel, whether they are advised of their rights, and whether the judge and jury are impartial.

This recourse to process may also occur where the goals are known, but the means to them is unknown. The areas of education and health care provide examples of this. While it is difficult to know what will make a student learn a specific skill, people generally agree on certain procedural aspects of teaching these skills. Some of these include that students should spend a certain amount of time in school, that they should have instruction from teachers, and that they should have graded exercises. Similarly, though it is impossible to know how to make a patient well, certain diagnostic procedures are commonly accepted and expected. Thus, process takes precedence over outcome in determining appropriate behavior.

The policy-making process is similar to the above examples. It is often unclear what policy goals should be pursued. Many people have strong opinions, but there is seldom widespread agreement. When there is widespread agreement on an objective—people should be literate; there should be fewer traffic accidents; the infant mortality rate should be lower; there should be less crime—there is little agreement on how to accomplish it.

As a result it is hard to specify or to evaluate the role that information and the producers of information should play in this process. It is possible, however, to specify procedures for producing information. One can specify that information should be produced, that it should be in the form of analysis, and that it should conform to expert standards (of course, expert standards are no more a given than are problems or solutions). One can specify which agencies should be involved and which particular agency should take the "lead" in producing the information. It is also possible to ask that information be produced on a given topic by a certain date.

These process rules do, in fact, regularize the work process for bureaucratic analysts. By requiring that many interests be represented in writing a paper, the rules also enable bureaucratic analysts to produce the particular and unique information that they contribute to the policy-making process. In addition, the requiring of these negotiations encourages greater sharing of information. This results in more people understanding the interests that are represented in the bureaucracy.

These rules, however, run directly contrary to the expectations established by the problem-solving perspective. They make the general case more important than the current one. They emphasize process over outcome. The way papers are written is more important than making sure that particular pieces of information are included in the papers. Obtaining all the necessary signatures is more important than putting the report in the hands of policy makers as quickly as possible.

For these reasons bureaucratic analysts tend to focus on the ways in which these routines obstruct the ends they have in mind. For instance, rather than seeing the concurrence process as a means of creating and sharing interpretations, they see it as a process that inhibits or prevents the analyst from providing important information to policy makers. One person's exasperated comment about government work is that "the review time is two orders of magnitude larger than the time to do the work" (field notes, 7/8/81). This comment makes clear that the "real work" does not include the review process.

Analysts do not see the policy-writing routine as a means of developing an inventory of shared interpretations that may be used when needed. Instead, they see it as a waste of time, because the way of thinking about the issue that has been proposed in the paper is not adopted and sometimes not even brought to the attention of policy makers. At one point, for instance, two analysts commented on how funny they thought it was to see the assistant secretary so excited about a particular study. They said that they had already been through it (had produced other similar studies of this topic) several times and they did not expect anything much to come of it (field notes 5/22/80). Another time, an analyst remarked that he was becoming increasingly cynical and disinterested. He noted, among other sources of these feelings, that he was writing the same memo that he had written three and one-half years ago—and several times in between (field notes, 4/23/81).

Instead of viewing their responsibilities for an issue as promoting the dissemination of information, analysts complain that they have to spend time tracking down information, obtaining support for projects, and establishing their position among others who deal with the same topic. One staff member, for instance, described the work bureaucratic analysts do by the phrases "lots of motion, not much of it forward" and "just chasing my tail" (field notes, 5/13/80).

Conclusion

Bureaucratic analysts tend to think of their work in terms of producing solutions for policy problems. They become discouraged, frustrated, and cynical when their analyses are not directly used in policy decisions. They see the procedures they must follow to produce information as preventing them from making a contribution. This focus is understandable. These people spend a lot of time working on a topic and feel that they have arrived at a good way of thinking about it (field notes, 5/6/80, 5/9/80). They naturally want policy makers to pay attention to their suggestions. In addition, they are committed to certain policy outcomes. This may be a consequence of having worked on the topic, or working on the topic may be a consequence of being committed to certain policy outcomes. In either case, they are likely to care about what policy makers decide and are therefore likely to want to have as much direct influence on that process as possible.

The problem-solving perspective encourages this way of thinking. It promises the very attractive possibility of directly influencing policies. The demoralizing effect of dashed hopes is, however, a high price to pay. The interpretive perspective, by contrast, offers a vision of the bureaucratic analyst's role that is much less glamorous. It is, however, much more true to the work they actually do and the context they work in. What it offers to analysts is a justification for valuing their work and respecting their contribution to policy making.

PART IV

Implications

CHAPTER 10

Bureaucratic Analysts
and Their Work

BUREAUCRATIC ANALYSTS have been portrayed as experts who use well-defined methods to produce analyses of policy problems (MacRae, 1981; Meltsner, 1980; Nagel, 1980). The primary purpose of their work according to this description is to help policy makers make decisions. Their analyses provide information about policy problems and may suggest possible solutions.

This description of the role makes it sound simple. It isn't. One set of complications is created by a professional ideal of objectivity. Under any circumstances this ideal is impossible to fulfill. An indeterminate amount of personal or organizational bias accompanies any analysis (Benveniste, 1972; Dahl, 1963). Additional tension is created by the need to respond to organizational pressures for the presentation of information with a specific bias. Analysts may use social science methods to reduce the subjective bias of their analyses. The organization, however, also imposes constraints on time and other resources. It specifies procedures to be followed and roles to be filled. These create incentives that favor some perspectives over others. This is an inevitable source of bias. Striking a balance between these two pressures is an important issue for the field of public policy (Meltsner, 1972; Schott, 1976; Wilensky, 1964).

While the balancing of these contrary pulls is important to the work of bureaucratic analysts, it is only one of the complications of the role they play in the policy-making arena. As the preceding chapters have shown, analysts not only provide technical and analytical information to help policy makers make decisions, but also develop interpretations of policy issues and negotiate agreement on these interpretations. Implicit in the negotiation process is the fact that they work between organizations. The agreements they negotiate are not only with representatives of other organizations, but also with the officials of their own organization. In a sense, they represent the interests of other organizations to their own organization and thus are boundary spanners as well as negotiators. This chapter discusses these two roles.

Bureaucratic Analysts as Negotiators

When analysts write papers, they produce interpretations of issues. They do this by including the facts and concerns that they see as relevant to understanding the issue they are writing about. Their choice of facts and concerns is determined by the way they think about and understand the issue. Bureaucratic analysts are constrained in their choice of facts and concerns in two ways that more independent analysts are not. First, bureaucratic analysts are members of organizations and are obliged to promote and protect the interests their organizations represent. In many cases the amount of choice the analysts have is very limited. Positions the organization has taken in the past on this issue or the preferences of an organizational official may almost completely determine what position the analyst takes. The second constraint is that analysts have to agree about the interpretation with other analysts representing other interests.

As a result of these constraints, much of the bureaucratic analyst's skill lies not in the choice of interpretations but in the ability to negotiate agreements on a given issue: to give up as much but not more than necessary; to know when agreement is really important; to protect the most crucial elements of the interests he or she represents. Negotiating these agreements requires both expertise and skill in using that expertise in order to achieve the best possible outcome.

Expertise

Three kinds of expertise are necessary for bureaucratic analysts to perform their jobs effectively. They are knowledge about the position being represented, about the substance of the issue being written about, and about the organizational context in which the work is being performed.

Knowledge of the Position. Negotiating for a position entails understanding what the position is. This seems straightforward. But knowing a position is not necessarily straightforward. Positions can have many nuances. The Department of Energy did, for example, support granting the right of eminent domain to coal slurry pipelines. It did not, however, support all legislation that granted this right; there were other aspects of the coal slurry issue to consider. In fact, the year before the testimony described in Chapter 4 was written, legislation that would have granted eminent domain to the pipelines was opposed by DOE because some of the other provisions were considered so rigid that they would have inhibited the ability of the pipelines to develop as a means of transporting coal. Thus, even if you can state the position very succinctly (e.g., we want to increase the likelihood of coal slurry development), you cannot translate that statement very easily into what positions a policy analyst should take on specific aspects of specific papers. Even in this case, the statement of the position is overly simplified, for the position was not to support the development of coal slurry pipelines at all costs. Other concerns had to be taken into consideration, such as the effect of the development on other forms of coal transportation or on the future development of coal as an energy source. This kind of knowledge develops over time as analysts become acquainted with the nuances of the issue, the interactions among these nuances, and the overall positions of the organization they represent.

Substantive Knowledge of the Issue. Bureaucratic analysts need substantive knowledge of the issue they are writing about. Substantive knowledge increases the analyst's ability to develop a better understanding of the issue. The more knowledge one has about the facts and concerns relevant to one's interests in the issue, the more likely one is to be able to include them in and thereby strengthen an interpretation.

Substantive knowledge is also useful in the negotiating process. It influences whose arguments are attended to and sometimes even who is included in the process. People who have little knowledge tend not to be taken seriously. For example, early in the process of writing the National Energy Transportation Study, one analyst was discounted as a possible contributor because he "didn't know much of anything." The people making this claim supported it by referring to an incident in which the analyst had said that water wasn't a problem for coal slurry pipeline production, which showed that the analyst indeed knew very little about the matter. Even though little of the National Energy Transportation Study dealt with coal slurry pipelines, the incident was used to discount any contribution to the report this analyst might make (field notes, 5/29/80).

Substantive knowledge can also help analysts expand their influence. People who have lots of substantive knowledge are generally respected, and their contributions to discussions are taken seriously. Analysts with particularly well-developed expertise may be invited to participate in writing or commenting on a report even when their organization is not on the concurrence list (Gregory's activities provide an example of this in week 5, Appendix B).

Arguments about substance are part of the negotiating process, and substantive expertise can be decisive in a dispute. For instance, if another analyst is arguing a point that you can prove is wrong, the point is unlikely to be included in the paper. Similarly, having more information than other analysts do can increase the likelihood of including a point that you want to make. Having pieces of information that other analysts are not aware of and have not taken into account in their arguments is particularly effective.

Substantive knowledge is also important in more mundane ways. For instance, in Chapter 5 there is an incident in which Gregory found a report on a topic related to his methanol report. Using information from that report saved a fair amount of money, which he then spent to expand other parts of his report. His substantive knowledge of the issue area beyond what he strictly needed to know in order to coordinate the methanol study helped him make the connection between the report he found and his own study.

Organizational Knowledge. Bureaucratic analysts need both knowledge of their own organization and of the organization of the analysts they deal with. They clearly need to work within the rules and norms of their own organization. They also can use these rules to their advantage. Deadlines or demands superiors make for accountability can be used to make claims and gain concessions in the substance of papers. Similarly, by knowing the rules and norms of the organizations of analysts they deal with, analysts can better judge the claims other analysts make and how far they can reasonably push them.

Bureaucratic analysts can use knowledge of their own organization and its procedures to insist upon the inclusion or exclusion of information and to increase their control over the paper-writing process. They often use organizational or procedural claims to influence the substance of agreements. The claim may simply be that "my boss won't buy this" or "this will never fly in my organization." A more complicated and compelling version of this claim involves relating other activities such as lawsuits, regulatory hearings, budget requests, or other reports that contradict some part of the interpretation being proposed. In this case, the analyst claims responsibility for maintaining consistency and insists that upper-level officials won't sign off on the paper in this form because of the inconsistency it would produce. (Of course, the analyst will, in all likelihood, be the person who informs the officials of the inconsistency; failure to do so would constitute a neglect of the analyst's duties.) Clearly the more extensive the analyst's knowledge of the activities and the predispositions of the organization's members, the more effective he or she can be in making these claims.

Knowledge of organizational procedure can also be used to increase control over the paper-writing process. This is presumably not an end in itself, but is undertaken to influence the substance of a paper. The railroad revenue adequacy case described in Chapter 4 provides some good examples of this use of procedural knowledge. The analysts from the Economic Regulatory Administration used their organization's need to account for money spent on consultants to gain greater control over the reports. Specifically, they claimed that they could not spend the money unless they obtained agreement from the other offices to use the information that would result from spending the money. The analysts from the policy office and the Office of the General

Counsel relied on their knowledge of procedure in dealing with this claim. First, they took a chance based on knowledge of their own organizations and past experience with the Economic Regulatory Administration that the claim being made was not strictly true. Second, they revived a letter written by a previous undersecretary that outlined the relationship among the three offices for producing papers of the sort they were currently working on. Some of this battle for control of the paper-writing process was waged on substantive grounds, but much of it was on procedural grounds. Analysts ill prepared to fight the procedural battle would have lost control of the substance of the paper.

Knowledge, both specific and general, about the organizations analysts deal with is also useful. As shown in the above example, it is helpful in discerning when other analysts are making credible claims and when their claims should be rejected. It is also useful in much more mundane circumstances. For instance, as discussed in Chapter 5, the information useful for doing one's job is not always readily available. People seldom refuse to give information, but they may simply not advertise its existence. Being a good analyst often involves being part detective. Being aware of the normal procedures and of deviations from them can provide clues as to the probable existence of information and where it is likely to be found. Daniel used this kind of knowledge in dealing with the report that was sometimes sent to him and sometimes sent elsewhere. His knowledge of the standard commenting procedure led him to realize when he first received the report that it was not the first time it had been sent out for comments. He was then able to find out who it had been sent to and keep track of it from then on. Though this is a trivial example, it is one that is repeated often and becomes important because of the number of times it occurs. The knowledge of the procedure required is not particularly elaborate or esoteric. What is important is an understanding of what is normal and a sensitivity to when and how deviations from this standard occur.

Use of procedures can also be important in encouraging people to find something they can agree to. For instance, in the National Energy Transportation Study, the Energy Secretary's special assistant was called at one point to put pressure on some of the participants to come to agreement. This is a ploy that cannot be used often, but can be effective when used appropriately.

Skill

Bureaucratic analysts use the expertise described above in negotiating. They use the knowledge to argue their positions persuasively and to compel their opponents to relinquish their positions without jeopardizing the possibility of reaching an agreement. They must be able to judge when they have asked for enough, too much, or too little and, likewise, when their opponents have asked for enough, too much, or too little. To be able to make such judgments, analysts must understand their own and their opponents' positions and have the substantive and procedural knowledge to understand what is reasonable. Thus, successful negotiating involves the use of the three forms of expertise.

Having the expertise, however, does not mean that an analyst will know how to negotiate interpretations. Negotiating involves combining this knowledge into smooth execution. While specific pieces of information can be learned through courses and books or from explanations of bosses and other analysts, learning to use the expertise is a different process. Negotiating interpretations of issues is a skill, which, like many skills, is more readily learned through practice than through verbal exchange (Polanyi, 1962).

A skill is a sequence of behavior in which each action is conditional upon the previous action or state. The skilled performer makes choices about what action to take next, but the choices are based on knowledge that is tacit and are not necessarily conscious (Nelson and Winter, 1982). Tacit knowledge and nondeliberative choices are important features of a skill. The freedom from conscious processing of information is what allows for a skilled performance.

Take driving a car as an example of a skill. The driver shifts gears as the car accelerates and decelerates. The appropriate gear is determined by what gear the car is currently in and whether the car is increasing or decreasing in speed. This is a programmatic sequence and usually occurs without any explicit knowledge or conscious choice except, of course, in the case of people who are learning to drive. Skilled drivers shift at the appropriate time without being aware that they should or even that they are doing it. They may simultaneously be listening or talking, reading street signs, and paying attention to traffic. It is, in fact, this ability to drive without paying conscious attention to the mechanics of driving that separates skilled from unskilled drivers.

As bureaucratic analysts write papers that contain negotiated agreements, they are practicing a skill. Writing policy papers, first of all, is programmatic. Actions taken are conditioned by the preceding action or state. As shown in Chapter 7, the steps taken in writing a paper are essentially reactive. The context defines the next appropriate step. In addition, there is a predictable pattern of acceleration of demands and pressures for agreement. Demands tend to be softly spoken at the beginning of the process. Pressures for acceleration tend to increase as work on the paper continues and as deadlines draw nearer.

Negotiating agreements also involves making nondeliberative choices on the basis of tacit or unspoken knowledge. As in the driving example, while some choices are very deliberate, many are not. Analysts depend on their tacit knowledge of communication, human relations, and the organizational and political context in order to make such choices as what words to use in an interpretation, how to understand what other analysts are saying, how much pressure to put on another analyst, and how hard to press for one's own position. In general, analysts behave in such a way that the negotiation continues without their being able to articulate the ways in which they are making that possible.

When a policy paper is written (or negotiated), many people with various levels of this skill perform simultaneously. The driving analogy is, again, apt. People can perform as drivers or as negotiators without having much skill. Some people never acquire much skill, and others seem to be born with it. Most people, however, learn it by practicing, and they get better with practice. Those people with more skill tend to achieve their ends more surely and more easily. It is also true, however, that no matter how much skill one has, one is dependent on other drivers or negotiators, since they form part of the context in which one must operate.

Bureaucratic Analysts as Boundary Spanners

The emphasis placed on the role of bureaucratic analysts as negotiators and as representatives of interests may encourage some to think about them as "hired guns." Bureaucratic analysts do represent their office's positions. There is an important distinction, however, between what they do and the work of a "hired gun." Bureaucratic analysts do not just represent their organization in negotiations; they also play a role in developing the position they represent.

When the office has not taken a position on an issue before, a bureaucratic analyst's role in developing a position may be large. Analysts can also influence the organization's position when that position is well established. Sometimes they do this by gathering information and doing analyses that lead them to different conclusions from those the organization has supported in the past or those their superiors currently support. Sometimes they come to new conclusions through the negotiating process. They may be persuaded by the arguments other analysts make, or they may become convinced that the best agreement they can negotiate entails some change in the organization's position. It is sometimes hard to separate these; what analysts believe is the best possible agreement has a lot to do with what they think about the issue.

Whether analysts change their minds about the issue because of arguments other analysts make or simply think that they have the best possible agreement, they need to convince their superiors to sign off on the paper. This means convincing their superiors that the way the issue is presented in the report is appropriate for their organization. In so doing, they are in the position of representing the interests of other organizations to their superiors. It is this particular feature of the job that makes bureaucratic analysts boundary spanners as well as negotiators.

The need for boundary spanning comes from the requirement for agreement or concurrence on the papers bureaucratic analysts write. Since almost all papers require this agreement and different offices and departments have the lead or the main responsibility for producing a report, the offices and departments are in a symbiotic interdependence (Scott, 1981). Every organization needs the cooperation of other organizations either now or in the near future. While department heads and other high-level officials do talk with one another, they do not have the time to work out detailed agreements on the numerous issues they are responsible for. They must rely on the analysts to do this. The analysts have both the time and the expertise to perform this role. Thus, they become liaisons between the interdependent organizations.

Thompson has noted that when boundary-spanning jobs occur in environments that are heterogeneous and shifting, they require the exercise of discretion (1967, p. 111). This characterization fits the environment in which bureaucratic analysts work. They write different kinds of papers on various aspects of the issues they are responsible for. The audience for the papers and the analysts and offices involved in writing the papers change. Discretion is required for dealing appropriately with these variations. Analysts must be able to make choices they can be reasonably sure will be supported by their superiors, either because a choice is consistent with organizational policy or because they can convince their superiors that it is the right choice to make. The three kinds of expertise discussed above are important to ensure this outcome.

Conclusion

Traditionally, bureaucratic analysts have been seen as people who provide analyses to help policy makers understand and solve policy problems. This role is in itself quite complicated (Meltsner, 1976). When bureaucratic analysts are viewed as being involved in the process of developing interpretations of issues, it becomes clear that the work they do involves not only being good analysts but also being skilled negotiators and intrepid boundary spanners. Currently, even those analysts who are trained in public policy schools are trained primarily in analytical techniques. Their training should also acquaint them with the role that they will play in the bureaucracy and should give them experience to prepare for this role.

The emphasis placed on the role of organizational interests and on the production of interpretations rather than solutions may appear to be contrary to training in analytical and statistical techniques. It is not. Analysts as negotiators and boundary spanners need to be able to develop their own analyses. They should, at least, be able to understand when statistical and other forms of data are being appropriately used. When they oversee or review studies in which data are gathered and analyzed, they should understand how to minimize subjective bias, and they should understand the consequences of the choices made about methods. Some analysts need only be concerned with such narrow technical issues. Most analysts, however, are and want to be in positions that require a broader range of expertise and skill. For these analysts an understanding of the substantive aspects of an issue and of the methods for gathering and analyzing data are necessary, but not sufficient.

Training in and an appreciation of the areas of expertise and skill discussed in this chapter are required for adequate preparation for the tasks bureaucratic analysts engage in. Currently, people develop the skill and expertise principally on the job. They have to in order to do a good job. Some knowledge and skill can only be developed in this way. A fine-grained sense of the organization's position on a particular issue, for instance, is very difficult to achieve outside of the organization. The next chapter discusses this feature of the work and the role that organizing plays in providing opportunities to learn. Much of what is necessary for being an effective analyst can, however, be learned outside the organization. Basic understandings about how organizations operate, about how to represent an interest, and about how to negotiate agreements out of conflict can be usefully discussed and practiced in classrooms and other settings outside the organization. Bureaucratic analysts develop these skills because the work they do requires them to. Training could enhance their effectiveness in the practice of these skills.

The problem-solving perspective emphasizes training and selecting analysts who are competent in the technical aspects of policy analysis. The interpretive perspective suggests that the abilities necessary for being a good bureaucratic analyst are much broader than that. An understanding of this perspective could help schools train analysts to be better prepared for this work. It would prepare them to be more effective negotiators and boundary spanners and also to expect the sort of work that most of them will, in fact, be doing. This will increase the attractiveness of the work for some and decrease it for others. On the whole, it should increase the value placed on the work by those who opt for these jobs and decrease disillusionment and cynicism.

CHAPTER 11

Organizing Analysts

STUDENTS OF ORGANIZATION have long noted that the
way work is structured is influenced by the type of work an organization has to do (Taylor, 1911; Gulick and Urwick, 1937; Simon,
Smithburg, and Thompson, 1950), the type of people who do
the work (Blau, 1968; Hall, 1968), and the environment in which
the work is performed (Thompson, 1967; Meyer and Rowan,
1977). More recently the argument has been turned around to
add that the structure of work influences what work is done and
how efficiently (Simon, 1981). This argument has been particularly strong among people thinking about information processing and decision making. They have found that the structure of
work within the organization affects what information is known
by whom (Cyert and March, 1963; Hammond, 1986), what influence the information can have (Taylor, 1984), how the environment is perceived and reinforced (Weick, 1979), and who participates in decisions and, as a result, what problems and solutions
are considered (Cohen, March, and Olsen, 1972; March and
Olsen, 1976). The perspective is echoed by students of bureaucratic politics who claim that what you think is important depends on where you are located in a decision-making structure
(Allison, 1971; Halperin, 1974). This study relies on similar no-
tions about the effects of the information-producing structure
on the policy-making process. This chapter explores two further
effects of the structure of work. One is how the way the work
is organized influences the contribution bureaucratic analysts
make to policy making. The other is how their work structure
affects their abilities to learn and perform the roles of negotiator
and boundary spanner discussed in the previous chapter.

Routines

Students of organization have proposed numerous ways of talking about organizational structure. One of the most common is to divide the structure into formal and informal. There is disagreement about what constitutes these structures. In general, one can say that the formal structure is that which is more permanent and consciously chosen while the informal structure is more variable and involves less conscious intervention (Scott, 1981). When organizational participants work, however, what matters are the patterns of behavior that structure their work. The origins of the structure make little difference. The patterns help them to establish what is going on and what they need to do. Thus, a focus on patterns of behavior and the organizational characteristics that help to shape them allows us to view the organization of work from the participant's perspective. The concept of routines establishes this focus.

Organizational routines are ways of organizing and performing work. They often involve interaction among organizational members. Routines are patterns of behavior that are constrained by rules, roles, and resources.* While we mostly think of fairly simple, predictable patterns when we talk about routines, the notion can be usefully extended to more complex patterns as well. More complex sets of behaviors may not be strictly predictable. There will, however, be a recognizable pattern of behavior that is characterized by a more or less explicit set of rules and relatively constant roles. These rules and roles constrain the behaviors in the pattern. They define a relatively limited set of behaviors appropriate for each participant given the current situation.

Participants in and observers of routines generally expect that the participants will mostly display appropriate behavior. While people may on occasion not behave appropriately—either because they do not agree about what constitutes appropriate behavior or because they choose not to conform to it—people more often do behave in ways consistent with established pat-

---

*See Allison, 1971 and Cyert and March, 1963 on standard operating procedures; March and Simon, 1958 on performance programs; and Nelson and Winter, 1982 on organizational routines.

terns. Thus, while the pattern is not a perfect predictor, it is a general guide to what is likely to happen. It is also helpful in understanding the reactions of other participants to what actually happens.

The existence of patterns of behavior and the influence of rules and roles on them is more clear when associated with concrete examples. The following section discusses the routines that seem most important to the production of information by bureaucratic analysts.

Routines for Producing Information

Three routines are prominent in the way the work of bureaucratic analysts is organized. They are the concurrence process, the paper-writing process, and the activities involved in being responsible for, or "taking care of," an issue. These routines are successively embedded in one another. The concurrence process is part of the paper-writing routine, and paper writing is part of taking care of an issue. Each of these ways of organizing work specifies a pattern of behavior with rules and roles. The following is a brief description of each of these routines.

The concurrence routine involves the circulation of written material to the offices on the concurrence list. One or more representatives from each of these offices is in some way assigned responsibility for reading the written material. These people evaluate whether or not their offices should concur on the document. They, in some way, inform the appropriate superiors of their determination. Once all the offices on the list concur, the process is over. If they do not all concur, measures are taken to alter the document in such a way that everyone can agree to support it. Rarely does the process simply collapse.

Being on the concurrence list is, in itself, a role. Associated with this role is the expectation that someone from each of the designated organizations will read and evaluate the document. The explicit rule is that every organization on the concurrence list will sign off on the document. The concurrence process also distinguishes between the organization with the lead and all of the other organizations on the list. It is generally expected that the lead organization will do most of the work and will be more invested in securing concurrence than the other organizations. There is also an assumption that the other organizations will put a reasonable amount of effort into finding enough common ground that agreement can be reached.

The concurrence routine is one part of the larger routine that I have called the paper-writing process. This routine starts with a request of some sort for a paper, often from superiors or from sources outside the organization, such as the White House or Congress. Reports may, however, be initiated from the lower levels of the organization. One office is given primary responsibility for the report. This office generates a document and sends it to the other offices on the concurrence list. These offices send back either their concurrence or their comments on how the report should be changed. Most of the time there is not perfect agreement on the report, and so representatives from the offices communicate in some way with one another about the report. These interactions become less intense as the representatives come to some sort of agreement. The paper-writing routine is over when the concurrence routine is concluded.

Since the concurrence process is so important to the paper-writing process, many of the rules and roles are the same. The office with the lead and everyone else on the concurrence list are distinct roles. Roles are generally more differentiated than this, however. For example, the policy office is often in charge of making sure that what a paper says is consistent with department policy. Similarly, the General Counsel's office checks the legality of what is being said. Other offices view the paper from their particular areas of expertise, which help define expectations. Offices usually take responsibility for providing information from their domain that is needed for the paper. Such information also is accorded special consideration as expertise, though there may well be disputes about the applicability and sometimes the veracity of particular pieces of information.

Organizing bureaucratic analysts' responsibilities according to broad topics specifies another pattern of behavior—"taking care of an issue." This pattern includes the expectation that when information on a topic is received in some part of the organization, it will be routed to the person or people who have responsibility for that topic. If it is not sent to the people taking care of the issue, they may seek out the information and assert a legitimate claim to it. This assertion is important to ensuring that similar information is sent to them in the future. Once the right people have received the information, they will respond to it in some way. Similarly, if others in the organization want someone to make a response to some information, they will contact the person with responsibility for the topic and that person will be included in some way in responding.

Writing and commenting on papers is part of taking care of an issue. An analyst taking care of an issue is also obliged to deal with problems that arise in connection with that issue. These include obtaining information about the issue, gaining support and approval for tasks relevant to the issue, and establishing a position among other people who deal with the issue. The specific behaviors required vary with the situation.

Having responsibility for an issue, itself, specifies a role. This person is the "coal-leasing person," that one the "methanol person," and so forth. These roles carry expectations with them. In general, one expects the coal-leasing person to know something about coal leasing and to be involved in papers and other tasks dealing with this topic. This person will represent the office when coal-leasing issues are raised and will establish himself or herself as the person to whom one should direct questions about this topic.

Effects of These Routines

Each of these routines has many consequences. Each influences the way bureaucratic analysts work and what work they do. Each of them affects the production of issue interpretations. The concurrence process determines who is involved in writing papers and encourages the combining of issue interpretations. The paper-writing routine produces inventories of these interpretations and keeps the inventories up to date. The organization of expertise according to topic areas produces a distribution of information that influences both the content and the dissemination of these interpretations.

The concurrence process almost completely determines who is involved in producing interpretations of particular issues. Occasionally representatives from offices that are not on the concurrence list are asked to contribute to a paper, but that is rare. As a result, the content of concurrence lists can be very important. If the paper is attended to by policy makers, the content of the concurrence list can have a direct effect on policy making. Only interests represented by offices on the list influence the interpretation contained in the paper. The interpretation reflects information about both the issue and the agreements possible among relevant interests. If the concurrence list does not properly designate relevant interests, policy makers may not receive important information.

As discussed in Chapters 8 and 10, the work bureaucratic analysts do has greater influence than reflected by the attention of policy makers. They affect the position their organization takes on an issue. They also influence the perceptions other analysts have of an issue, and these analysts influence their organizations' positions. Thus, analysts play a role that potentially has quite broad influence. The flow of this influence is largely determined by the content of concurrence lists.

The paper-writing routine ensures that there is a constant flow of papers on a broad range of issues. This flow is important both for providing information to policy makers and for promoting more general development of issue interpretations. The paper-writing routine makes it more likely that the information in a paper is kept up to date. It also provides opportunities for renegotiating and updating agreements. Sometimes this renegotiation results in less agreement than before. Often, however, what has already been agreed upon is taken as given, and the analysts are able to focus their attention on conflicts that have not yet been resolved.

The practice of analysts having broad responsibility for, or "taking care of," issues is the routine that probably has the largest impact on the work bureaucratic analysts do and, as a result, on issue interpretations. This is, in part, because most, if not all, of what an analyst does is defined by this responsibility. With few exceptions, the way of organizing responsibility for tasks in the policy office of the Department of Energy and among other analysts I encountered was to distribute responsibility for issues. That is, people were assigned to an issue, and they performed whatever tasks were associated with it; as discussed in

Chapter 6, analysts also expand their responsibilities by creating more tasks. The issues were not necessarily assigned to people who were experts in the area. In fact, many people working in the policy office had no prior expertise in energy issues at all (in my sample, only 19 of 34 policy analysts had experience in the energy field before joining the department). However, people quickly develop expertise as they perform the tasks required by their assignments.

Not all offices are organized in this manner. A few offices distributed tasks according to who was least busy when the task required attention. This has the advantage of smoothing out the amount of work each person has to do at any one time, but it is possible only when the responsibilities of the office as a whole are sufficiently specialized that the staff members share the relevant body of expertise.

While the delineation of responsibility is, like the definition of interests, a matter of interpretation in most offices, there was agreement that the responsibilities of staff members were relatively separate. The Office of Coal and Synthetic Fuels, for example, is responsible for issues ranging from coal leasing, export, and transportation to the development and impacts of synthetic fuel production. A person responsible for one of these issues has little knowledge that is relevant to other issues. In this case, issues are allocated to staff members. They then specialize and develop the expertise needed to perform the tasks associated with the issue (however, some overlap occurs so that people can fill in for one another during vacations and sick leave).

This division of labor by issue leads analysts to perform many different tasks and engage in many different activities associated with these tasks. It also makes it necessary for them to confront many of the types of problems we have seen can be part of their work and provides them with opportunities for expanding their responsibilities. Through these means they are able to develop expertise, increase their visibility, and enhance their reputations, all of which are necessary for career mobility.

These activities also enable analysts to influence the interpretation of issues that are contained in policy papers. As shown in Chapter 8, their efforts to confront problems and expand their responsibilities affect who participates in report writing, what information is available for inclusion in papers, and what information is actually contained in a particular paper.

Routines as Motivators

One of the interesting features of these routines is their ability to organize work and produce results despite the fact that the participants in these routines do not appear to value or even recognize the outcomes and often specify other outcomes they would prefer to have. Still people continue to participate in the routines and appear to be unable to change either the routine or the result. This section explores how the notion of routine can help to explain this situation.

Organizational routines are complex sets of interlocking behaviors, held in place through common agreement on the relevant roles and expectations. These generally unspoken agreements about what it means to be the coal-leasing person or to have the lead on a particular paper are powerful constraints on behavior. If any one actor does not perform within the limits of the other actors' expectations, the latter will pressure the former in more or less subtle ways to conform. If the coal-leasing person does not provide the information needed about leasing, then others who want that information but are not experts in the area will apply pressure to get it. If offices on the concurrence list do not sign off on a document, the office with the lead will pressure them to do so, and the lead office will in turn receive pressure from hierarchical superiors or the organization that requested the document. Hierarchical superiors may even pressure offices on the concurrence list if the lead office is not successful.

Any particular set of agreements about rules and roles is a sort of equilibrium satisfying the demands of many different parties. Nelson and Winter (1982) have referred to this as a "truce," but the adversarial metaphor is not necessary to capture the complexity of the situation. Many organizations or parts of organizations must coordinate their behavior in such a way that each can cope adequately with the pressures and constraints it has to satisfy. While there may be many possible solutions to such a problem, they are not necessarily easy to find. Even if one of the participants finds a new solution that will satisfy the constraints of all parties, the problems of persuading everyone else that this would be a beneficial change may still be considerable. The actors' interdependence and abilities to pressure one another to conform combined with the difficulties in finding new solutions make the persistence of the routine likely even if the participants are not convinced of its value. One study of routines (Cohen, 1985) has used a computer model to simulate this process and to illustrate the persistence of standard operating procedures as a result of the interlocking nature of the behavior that produces them.

Efficiency

While the way of organizing bureaucratic analysts described in this chapter contributes to the process of issue interpretation, there is no automatic reason to believe that it is a particularly good or efficient way. In fact, one cannot help but notice that many of the tasks bureaucratic analysts do are pretty mundane. It hardly seems efficient for highly educated professionals to be doing things like tracking down information or finding out why a contract has not been signed.

Reasonable observers of bureaucratic analysts might suggest that a more efficient use of government resources would result if experts were hired to negotiate agreements on a case-by-case basis while less expensive personnel performed the administrative tasks. In other words, one might suggest that paper writing could be more effectively provided by a market than by a hierarchy (see Williamson, 1975 and 1981 for a discussion of the different advantages of markets and hierarchies). Consultants are hired in some cases to work on papers and help negotiate agreements, but much of what bureaucratic analysts do could not be performed by an outside consultant with no vested interest in the outcome. Furthermore, much of what is being accomplished would be lost if this procedure were followed. Since the paper-writing process involves the production of negotiated interpretations and not simply technical solutions, bureaucratic analysts are, as we have noted, negotiators and boundary spanners as well as analysts more narrowly defined. Both of these roles require two things. One is practice to develop skill. The other is discretion. Having in-house analysts who are responsible for virtually all the tasks associated with an issue fulfills both of these needs.

Taking care of an issue provides the bureaucratic analysts with many opportunities to practice and develop skill in negotiating agreements. Performing the tasks that come up gives the analysts chances to increase their expertise and to try out new arguments and new ways to make old arguments. Analysts can become better at dealing with the particular issue and with the people or offices involved with the issue.

Taking care of an issue also provides many opportunities to develop an understanding of the values supported by the officials or the organization and by organizational actions. Analysts understand the position of their organization because they have been involved in developing it and because they have been socialized on a daily basis to the values that underlie the position. They learn from being involved in paper writing and other tasks and by interacting with their superiors around these tasks. They may have been reprimanded for giving in too easily or for being too intransigent. They may have been praised for negotiating an agreement to which their superiors could readily sign their names. They learn from talking with their colleagues about other agreements and the difficulty of achieving those agreements.

Not only are these conditions important for effectively engaging in the production of information, but they are also part of the effect of the process. Both development and dissemination are essential to the process of issue interpretation. The repetition that provides practice also enables analysts to promote the argument(s) they are making to new audiences or to make them more convincingly to the same audience. Since no report is definitive, so long as the analyst stays with the same issue she or he always has another opportunity to develop better arguments or better ways to argue.

The ability to exercise discretion allows the analyst the freedom to go beyond the positions established by other analysts or by upper-level officials. It allows them to make new agreements that push the interpretation process in new directions. Without this ability the roles of negotiator and boundary spanner would not be very meaningful, and the process of issue interpretation would tend to stagnate.

People hired to participate in a single report-writing incident may have very good knowledge of the substance and politics of the issue. They cannot, however, have the understanding of the organizational context in which the report is written that in-house analysts have. Only in rare cases do they have the experience to understand the limits of an acceptable agreement. Furthermore, they would not provide the continuity in developing interpretations that people who remain inside the bureaucracy almost inevitably do.

Limitations

The foregoing discussion points out some of the advantages of the way work is organized for the roles bureaucratic analysts play in the production of information. However, there are some serious questions about this means of organizing. They pertain to whether this way of organizing is efficient for what is accomplished and whether what is accomplished is appropriate.

While the way that bureaucratic analysts are organized has some important advantages that should not be overlooked, it seems unlikely that having highly paid professionals spend a substantial amount of their time performing mundane tasks is efficient. It seems likely that without losing the advantages, the structure could be modified to be more efficient. For instance, administrative assistants may be able to perform many of these tasks with little or no loss in terms of the development of the analysts' abilities.

The knottier issue involves the amount of power and autonomy this structure gives to analysts. They have a great deal of control over what papers they pay more or less attention to. They often have influence over what features of issues come to the attention of their bosses and higher officials in the organization. In some instances, they have a substantial effect on the interpretation contained in a paper and, consequently, on the position the organization supports.

Such power and autonomy are not necessarily inappropriate. They are features of many jobs in the lower levels of bureaucracies (Lipsky, 1980). They are, however, features that must be taken into consideration in both training and organizing. Police forces (Skolnick, 1975) and the forest service (Kaufman, 1967) both provide examples of the ways in which organizations can use selection processes, formal and informal socialization, and career incentives to regulate the exercise of discretion. These means of control should also be considered for bureaucratic analysts. A greater degree of professionalization among analysts is another means of control that has been suggested (Meltsner, 1980; Quade, 1970).

Conclusion

The interpretive perspective emphasizes several features of the work of bureaucratic analysts that should be taken into consideration in the way that work is organized. The routines that currently organize their work allow them to produce and disseminate interpretations of issues and to develop the abilities necessary for engaging in the production of these interpretations. These features of the routines are important for bureaucratic analysts effectively to promote the arguments important to the interests they represent. More efficient means of organizing can almost surely be developed, but it is important that these features and their effects be appreciated and considered when changes are proposed.

CHAPTER 12

The Production of Information

THIS STUDY has drawn together three strands of existing thought. One of them is that issue interpretation is part of decision making (Cohen, March, and Olsen, 1972; Weick, 1979) and of the policy-making process (Lindblom, 1968; Lynn, 1978; Smith, 1984). Lindblom, for example, notes the need to define policy problems: "Policy makers are not faced with given problems. Instead they have to identify and formulate their problems" (1968, p. 13).

The second strand is that information produced by analysts contributes to the policy-making process by influencing the way issues are understood (Lindblom and Cohen, 1979; Weiss, 1980; Weiss and Bucuvalas, 1980). Weiss has described the process as "knowledge creep." She claims that research supplies the context from which ideas, concepts, and choices derive and that it provides a "background of empirical generalizations that *creep* into deliberations" (1980, p. 381).

The third strand is that positive social action can occur without being consciously coordinated or organized (Elster, 1983; Hayek, 1945; Lindblom, 1965; Merton, 1936). In his exploration of these unanticipated consequences, Merton points out that "in short, undesired effects are not always undesirable effects" (1936, p. 895). Lindblom has explored this notion as a part of the policy-making process. He argues that mutual adjustment is a means of noncoordinated policy making that produces coordinated outcomes. He suggests that some outcomes are more easily attained through this means than they would be through conscious coordination. Elster takes this line of thought one step further by discussing outcomes that can *only* be by-products of intentional action and never the direct product.

These ideas have been used to make sense of the observations of bureaucratic analysts at work that form the basis for the study. Particular attention has been paid in these observations to the context in which bureaucratic analysts work, to the way the context influences how their work is organized, and to the effects of this organization on the work they produce.

These observations have led to a new way of describing the contribution bureaucratic analysts make to policy making. This contribution is indirect and diffuse. It supports the gradual development of understandings and interpretations of issues. As bureaucratic analysts work at the tasks associated with producing information, they contribute to the development of issue interpretations. They promote the interests that they and their offices represent when they negotiate with other analysts about what facts and concerns should be included in a paper. They influence the way other analysts perceive the issue through these negotiations. They influence the way officials in their organization perceive the issue through their recommendations to concur or not to concur. Other tasks that support paper writing help the analysts to develop better arguments and to enlarge their sphere of influence. This increases their opportunities to persuade both other analysts and their superiors and helps them to increase the effectiveness of their persuasive efforts.

This way of understanding what bureaucratic analysts do is consistent with the notion of producing solutions to problems. In fact, the interpretation of issues is a necessary part of decision making and of the policy-making process. Interpretations influence what policy makers perceive as problems and what they see as appropriate solutions. However, thinking that what bureaucratic analysts do is provide solutions to problems or even define what the problem is captures only a part of their contribution to policy making.

A Comparison with the Price System

The process of information production described here has two characteristics of particular interest. One is its effect of moving information through the organization or structure involved in producing it. Many pieces of information held by many individuals are disseminated to other individuals who can use the information. The process does not simply result in reports to decision makers, but also results in a much broader dissemination and discussion of ideas about how to understand issues. The second characteristic is that the process was apparently not designed to produce this broad dissemination of information. Bureaucratic analysts, their bosses, observers, and policy makers are aware of the process as a means of providing information to decision makers. There is no indication that it is appreciated as a means of sharing information among bureaucratic analysts and, thus, among units within the bureaucratic structure.

These two characteristics are similar to the price system described by Hayek. In his essay on the use of knowledge in society, he suggests that the price system solves what he describes as the fundamental economic problem. The problem is to find a method to make widely available knowledge that "never exists in concentrated form but solely as the dispersed bits of incomplete and contradictory knowledge which all the separate individuals possess" (Hayek, 1945 / 1984, p. 212). The price system summarizes and communicates information contributed by all the people who take part in it (i.e., all those who buy and sell).

This system operates not through conscious design but through serving the ends of the individuals who contribute to it (Hayek, 1978 / 1984, p. 258). In this regard, too, it is like the bureaucratic production of information described in this book. The analysts participating in the process are not intent on informing one another but on defending the interests they represent and having their points of view reflected in the written reports they participate in producing.

One feature that distinguishes these two systems is the type of information contained and produced in them. Hayek points out that the causes of effects in the price system are not important for people reacting to them. Only the size of the effect is relevant information. This is true because the end this information serves is to decide whether to take a particular action (to buy or not). By contrast, the information produced by and contained in the process described in this book is useful for developing understandings of issues. For this purpose the causes or perceived connections between causes and effects are exactly the kind of information that is necessary.

Relevance to Other Settings

The content of this study is most directly relevant to the interpretation of issues in public policy and to the role of bureaucratically employed analysts in that process. However, several ideas developed in this book are relevant to any bureaucratically structured organization (i.e., having a hierarchy and delineated functions) confronting issues of ambiguity or equivocality.

First, issues of ambiguity cannot be resolved in the way uncertainty can. Resolution is a matter of agreement rather than proof. To the extent that resolution occurs, it comes from shared understandings, not factual information. Understanding these issues involves exploring the many conceptions of them and the interconnections among these conceptions.

Second, the organization of information production influences the type of information that is available to decision makers. In this case the organization compels analysts to combine their points of view and to engage in a process of confronting each other's point of view. This process influences what they know, what they believe, and what they communicate to decision makers.

Third, information production within an organization does more than simply funnel information to decision makers. It can induce broader understandings of an issue at many levels of the organization. The process of producing information is a learning process. People do not simply contribute what they know. What they know changes as a result of their participation in the process, and the way the process is structured influences how much of this learning occurs.

These observations are important for organizations that deal in areas of ambiguity where it is impossible simply to communicate the right answer or the right way to proceed. In such organizations the employees' understandings of an issue or situation will influence their abilities to act appropriately. A means of information production that allows them to understand more fully the complexity of issues relevant to their work will help them to perform better. It will help them in seeking new information, in representing their positions, and in proposing new actions.

An Interpretive Perspective on Policy Analysis

Recently, many people have been calling for a more phenomenological, interpretive, contextual, or hermeneutic approach to policy analysis (Dryzek, 1982; Healy, 1986; Jennings, 1983; Torgerson, 1986b). There are similarities between the arguments these people are making and the argument made in this book. In both cases the need for interpretation is associated with the ill-specified nature of policy problems (see Rittel and Webber, 1973 for a good discussion of this feature of policy issues). There is an emphasis in both arguments on the importance of acknowledging that an issue can be perceived in many different ways and that these perceptions are essential information for policy making. However, the discussion in this book differs in several key ways.

First, the argument here is an organizational argument. It is restricted to the analyses that occur within a bureaucratic structure. The process described in this book could not be undertaken by an analyst working alone. The interpretation that emerges from this process develops in the "system" or organization rather than in the heads of analysts. The interpretations to which bureaucratic analysts contribute take place outside the control of any single analyst or group of analysts. They occur through the combining of perspectives proposed by analysts and others.

By contrast, the interpretive approach called for by many is an individual approach to analysis. Dryzek, for example, discusses six forms of analysis that are appropriate in different circumstances and that a single analyst can use to approach an issue. One of these is the hermeneutic approach, which, as Dryzek describes it, is similar to the method used in this book to make sense of the work that bureaucratic analysts do. This individual approach to interpretation is not incompatible with the organizational approach. It is possible, for instance, that the contribution a bureaucratic analyst would make to an organizational interpretation would be based on a hermeneutic analysis.

The emphasis on organizational interpretation leads to attention to the bureaucracy and its structure. The bureaucracy as it is divided and subdivided into units embodies the interests that are represented in the organizational interpretations. The perspective in this book draws attention to the importance of the bureaucratic structure as a means of promoting interests. The fit of this structure with the interests in the society should be seriously considered. While bureaucratic analysts do make some efforts to find out about the concerns of the individuals and groups whose interests correspond to those promoted by their organization, they are primarily bound by the organizational definitions of interests.

The individual approach to interpretation is not bound by organizational context. The analysts envisioned by those suggesting this approach are free to deal directly with the interests as they exist in society. Analysts so free from organizational constraints may be rare. However, increased legitimacy of this approach to policy analysis may help to break down some of the barriers that separate organizations representing interests from people who have the interests.

The second difference is that people calling for interpretive policy analysis attribute much more potential for control over policy outcomes to the analysis than is envisioned here. Both Dryzek and Torgerson, for instance, discard the phenomenological or interpretive approach in favor of a hermeneutic or critical one because of the legitimacy of evaluation and recommendations for change in the latter (Dryzek, 1982; Torgerson, 1986a). In many contexts this is an important distinction. In this one, however, it is only important if you believe that analysts have control over what is done with, and as a result of, the information they produce. The argument in this book is that they do not and that interpretation occurs precisely because no one has that kind of control.

The final difference involves the perspective on the need for interpretation. An appeal for more interpretation in policy making implies that interpretation is a discretionary activity. The claim here is that interpretation is already happening and is necessarily happening. It is not something that we have to convince people to do. It is something that we cannot help but do because of the nature of the world, in general, and policy making, in specific. If the world were given to us in a more orderly fashion, then we would not have to interpret. But it is not, and we do. What we must do is recognize how this need for interpretation influences and is influenced by the context of the work and the way in which work is organized. We must entertain some difficult questions about what kinds of influences are appropriate or inappropriate and how we can encourage the appropriate ones and discourage the inappropriate ones. Through this book I have tried to start that process.

Appendixes

Case Studies of the Report-Writing Process

Coal Slurry Pipeline Testimony

Every year of the Department of Energy's (DOE) existence and for several years before that, legislation was introduced into Congress to authorize the granting of federal eminent domain for coal slurry pipelines. Two groups had always opposed the legislation. One group consisted primarily of railroads and railroad labor groups who believed that slurry pipelines would reduce rail coal shipments and profits. The other group consisted primarily of farmers and ranchers in the arid western states who feared that the pipelines, once built, would have the rights to water usage to the point of endangering the region's ability to provide for their water needs. Over the years the legislation had included increasingly strong wording regarding the maintenance of all water rights at the state level.

In the summer of 1980, DOE had been asked to testify before Congress on the slurry pipeline issue. The department was generally favorably disposed to the development of coal slurry pipelines and had in the past supported eminent domain legislation. That year there were several versions of this legislation, and some were felt to have such constraining use and ownership restrictions that they would actually hinder rather than help the development of coal slurry pipelines. The staff involved in this issue from several parts of the department (Office of the General Counsel, Resource Applications, Economic Regulatory Administration, the policy office, Office of Environment) came together and agreed on a seven-point statement that could be used as the basis for comments on any of the pieces of legislation. The seven points covered such things as eminent domain, water rights, environmental concerns, and use and ownership restrictions. When testimony on a specific piece of legislation was called for, the appropriate staff would write the testimony using the seven points and drawing particular attention to the points most relevant to that piece of legislation.

The Participants

The major administration participants in the slurry pipeline issue in 1981 were the Department of Energy (DOE), the Department of Interior (DOI), the Department of Transportation (DOT), and the Interstate Commerce Commission (ICC). Within DOE, the main organizational participants were the policy office, Fossil Energy (which had absorbed Resource Applications in the 1981 reorganization), the Office of the General Counsel, and the Secretary's office.

The Process

In the summer of 1981, the DOE staff became aware that slurry pipeline legislation would again be introduced and that DOE would again be asked to testify. This was the first year of the Reagan administration, and many policies had changed. Even where the actual position taken had not changed, the presentation usually had. None of the staff had any question about the DOE's continued support for granting eminent domain for coal slurry pipelines. They gathered to reconstruct the presentation of the previous year's seven-point statement.

Later that summer, the issue was taken up by an interdepartmental group called the Cabinet Council working group. Under Reagan, administration-wide positions were determined by a subset of the cabinet, in this case, by the Cabinet Council on Natural Resources and Environment (hereafter referred to as the Cabinet Council). Some issues—among them, the slurry pipeline issue—that had previously required only department-wide consensus now needed administration-wide agreement. The Cabinet Council would have to determine what position the administration would take before the departments could testify at the Congressional hearings.

The working group, composed of high-level officials and staff from the DOI, the DOE, the DOT, and the ICC, among others, served as a sort of staff to the council, preparing information and preliminary positions. The group considered four aspects of the slurry pipeline issue, generally felt to be the key issues in this area: federal eminent domain, water rights, economic regulation, and ownership restrictions. The working group met many times to discuss the issues. Five or six versions of an options paper were written, read, and reviewed by members of the group and by others not participating in the group who were knowledgeable about the issue. Finally, a meeting aimed at resolving the issues was held on August 14. In this meeting no one opposed the granting of federal eminent domain to coal slurry pipelines; everyone agreed that the states should maintain complete control over water rights; there was general agreement that there should be some form of economic regulation of slurry pipelines and that the ICC was the appropriate regulatory body. The only issue left unresolved was whether ownership restrictions were necessary or appropriate. While the Cabinet Council working groups were not considered to be final policy-making bodies, the status of the participants and the care with which the working papers were developed indicates that the participants intended their work to pave the way for a speedy resolution of the issues and a determination of policy by the Cabinet Council itself.

A few weeks later, on September 3, the Cabinet Council met for the first time on this issue. The outcome surprised many who had taken part in or followed the progress of the working group. The meeting came to a standstill on the granting of federal eminent domain. The other three aspects of the issue were not even discussed. Though the proceedings of the Cabinet Council are not public, word leaked out that Secretary James Watt (Department of Interior) was the major opponent of federal eminent domain and that Secretary James Edwards (Department of Energy) was the major proponent. A special assistant to Secretary Edwards later confirmed this information. This was significant to the DOE staff because it meant that when the issue was raised again, Secretary Edwards would be the main spokesperson for eminent domain. It would be the responsibility of the DOE staff to prepare him for this position.

Neither the Cabinet Council nor the working group met on this issue during the rest of September. An analysis of the four aspects of the issue was written in the DOE policy office. The paper was started on September 11 and sent to the Secretary's office October 14.

The next Cabinet Council meeting was supposed to resolve the disagreement over authorizing federal eminent domain for coal slurry pipelines. A rumor circulated that the president would attend this meeting. If this rumor was true, it would constitute quite a change for the people who habitually worked on this issue. It had never been a dead issue, but it had never been a particularly live one either. There had been a steady but not large amount of work to do on it. The work had rarely involved anyone higher than an office director. Until the recent events, the issue had been characterized by very little controversy or visibility.

A Cabinet Administration Staffing Memorandum confirmed the rumor. The main purpose of this memorandum was to transmit a copy of an options paper written to inform the president about the issue. Several agencies were asked to review the document to see if it represented the views of that agency before it was sent to the president. Comments were to be sent to the deputy assistant to the president by noon on October 16. Though dated more than a week earlier, the memo did not arrive at DOE until the morning of October 16, a little more than three hours before the deadline for comments.

The reaction by participants in the policy office in DOE was that the memorandum did not represent the views of the agency. This is hardly surprising given that the memo (hereafter referred to as the Watt memo) was signed by Secretary Watt, who had taken the opposite position from DOE in the September 3 meeting. That morning two memoranda were written by the division director and staff member in the Fossil Fuel Division of the policy office in response to the Watt memo. One of these suggested two pages of points that should be added to the Watt memo. The second was a DOE version of the Watt memo in the standard one-page form for a memorandum to President Reagan. Both of these memoranda were completed and ready to transmit to the White House shortly after the noon deadline. They could not be sent, however, without going through the proper channels. Because of the high-level involvement in this case, the proper channels included the Secretary's office. No one was available from this office until early in the afternoon. When someone was available, this person determined that rather than send the documents that had been prepared, he would call the White House and ask them to extend the deadline. He called, the deadline was retracted, and no specific deadline was put in its place.

With more time available, attention was focused on changing the Watt memo so that both DOE and DOI would find it acceptable. Between October 17 and October 29, the policy staff member, working closely with her division director, produced almost daily versions of this memorandum. Copies of each new version of the memo were delivered to the various levels of hierarchy in policy and to the relevant people in the Secretary's office. Comments were transmitted from time to time, usually coming down through the layers of hierarchy. A couple of times it was reported that a representative from the Secretary's office took the latest version of the memo to the White House staff member in charge of making sure that a memo acceptable to all parties was produced.

During this time several documents were supplied to the policy office to help improve the quality and the validity of the arguments being made. For instance, documents regarding different aspects of state and federal eminent domain authority written by two Washington law firms were sent from the Office of the General Counsel. Revisions of the Watt memo by the special assistant to the Attorney General (Justice Department, which also favored eminent domain) and by the special assistant to the DOE General Counsel were also received.

One letter received during this time provided a new perspective on the Watt memo. This was a letter from a Washington law firm, which referred to an attached memo as the "Boggs memo." The attachment was identical to, though dated earlier than, what has been referred to here as the Watt memo. Boggs was the person in the White House who was coordinating the current effort to produce a document acceptable to all. The indication from the letter was that he had written the original document that had not been acceptable to DOE. Thus, his neutrality in the ongoing process came into question. On October 29 a new version of the memorandum was sent from the White House. Boggs was identified as the author of this one. Many of the arguments DOE had made had been incorporated into this final draft.

The next exercise was preparing Secretary Edwards for the Cabinet Council meeting. A meeting of the assistant secretary of Fossil Energy, the director of the policy office, the general counsel, and the special assistant to the Secretary, along with staff members from these offices, was held. The primary purpose of this meeting was to make sure that everyone was on the same track so that when the Secretary asked questions in the briefing, he would not get several different answers. After a general discussion of the issues, tasks needing to be completed before the briefing were allocated. Fossil Energy was to provide some technical information. The policy office would provide the statements that the Secretary would make during the Cabinet Council meeting.

As mentioned earlier, the Secretary of Energy would be the primary proponent of granting federal eminent domain to coal slurry pipelines. This would put him in a spotlight for which the staff needed to prepare him. At one point the special assistant to the Secretary indicated that Watt would be out of town for the next Cabinet Council meeting at which this issue would be discussed. In this case Secretary Edwards would be the chair of the meeting. This would increase the importance of his preparation. On the chance that this might occur, briefing documents were prepared as if it were true. This preparation culminated in a 45-minute meeting at which the Secretary received the documents and asked a few questions about the issue. With this, the possibility of having any more influence over the determination of the issue was out of the hands of the people who had been working on it.

The next Cabinet Council meeting on this issue was scheduled for 10:30, November 5. The president attended, and Secretary Watt (DOI) chaired the meeting. The issue paper distributed prior to the meeting was the October 29 Boggs draft now dated November 1, 1981, and signed by Watt. The next day relevant DOE staff learned that the president had not made a decision but had chosen to think about it for a little while.

The DOE staff now turned their attention back to the task that had been the impetus for the whole exercise, preparing testimony for the Congressional hearing, now scheduled for November 17. This hearing already had been postponed once because of the lack of an administration position. Either the assistant secretary for Fossil Energy or the policy office director would be giving the testimony. The staff members in both offices usually worked together to write testimony regardless of who was going to present it. Writing testimony was usually a routine procedure. This case was clearly different, however. The DOE was expected to articulate the same position as the rest of the administration. Since no one knew what the administration position was, no one knew what the DOE position was. This made writing the testimony a little more difficult than usual.

The policy office and Fossil Energy staff members met on November 9. They had waited longer than usual hoping that the president would make a decision. As no decision was forthcoming and both people were aware that it takes a fair amount of time to get anything written, typed, proofed, corrected, and cleared, they determined, first, to write a background section that could be used regardless of what position was taken and, second, to write three main bodies of the testimony. One would be for eminent domain; one would be against; one would take no stand. This last possibility was included on the chance that no decision had been made by the time of the hearing.

On arriving at work Monday morning, the day before the testimony would be given, the policy staff member learned from the Fossil Energy staff member that the president had made a decision Friday evening, November 13, to oppose federal eminent domain for coal slurry pipelines. A meeting was scheduled that morning to brief the assistant secretary for Fossil Energy, who turned out to be the person giving the testimony.

This meeting was smaller, with a higher proportion of staff members, than the last several meetings concerning this issue. The first issue that was raised was that DOE might not have to testify at all. A call had been made from the office of the assistant secretary of Fossil Energy to the scheduling staff of the Congressional committee requesting that the Department of Interior be allowed to give the testimony for the administration. Originally both DOE and DOI had been scheduled to speak. Since only one position could be presented, however, and Secretary

Watt would be presenting that position, the assistant secretary saw no reason that he should go and say the same thing. Furthermore, he would be in the uncomfortable position of defending a position he had not endorsed and having to answer questions about why DOE had changed its stand on the issue. For the rest of the meeting participants posed questions to the assistant secretary of the type they assumed the committee members would ask the following day if he testified.

By noon that day the scheduling staff of the committee had called back to say that DOE did not have to testify.

Railroad Revenue Adequacy Statement

In this case there was considerable uncertainty about whether the participants would be able to resolve their conflicts enough to produce a report at all. The fact that they did manage to produce a signed document appears to be driven by two features of the process. One is that the office that had the lead on this report believed that it was very important to produce it. The second is that the participants in this process had a long history of struggle over the production of similar papers. As a result, even though the other participants were not particularly convinced of the importance of this paper, they were unwilling to relinquish their control over the process.

Background

The Staggers Rail Act of 1980 (the Act) was enacted by Congress October 15, 1980. The Act stated that the Interstate Commerce Commission (ICC) would establish regulations regarding several specific issues that were left unresolved by the legislation. What constitutes an adequate revenue level, how to determine market dominance, whether and to what extent "product competition" should be used to determine the "unreasonableness" of rates, the formulation of a methodology for determining the "cost recovery percentage," and what rules to establish concerning publication of contract information were the rulings of particular significance for coal transportation. Since these phrases were used in the Act, final regulations needed to be established before the Act would have any meaning. The Act specified that the decisions must be made within 180 days of enactment.

To establish a regulation, first a Notice of Proposed Rulemaking is published in the Federal Register. In this case, determining an adequate revenue level, the notice gave some background information and made a proposal. There was a discussion about why this particular proposal was chosen. There was also a concurring and a dissenting opinion from two commissioners. The notice told when statements about the regulation were due and where to send them. It also gave names and telephone numbers of people to call for more information.

After the notice appears in the Federal Register, there is a public commenting period. In this case this period was 45 days from the date the Notice of Proposed Rulemaking appeared on December 3, 1980, or January 17, 1981. As it turned out, this was a Saturday, so the deadline was pushed forward to the next Monday, January 19. The notice stated that there would be no extensions of this period because of the short time limits imposed by the Staggers Rail Act.

After statements are received, the Commission reviews them and makes a final determination. There is, of course, always legal recourse after the decision is made. Filing statements during this period, however, is seen as an important step and may even be necessary to establishing legal standing for any later legal actions.

The Participants

Three offices of the Department of Energy (DOE) were involved in these proceedings. They were the Economic Regulatory Administration (ERA), the Office of the General Counsel, and the policy office. Decisions about what proceedings to be involved in were to be made by the heads of these three offices. Once the decision to file a statement was made, the General Counsel's Office, in coordination with ERA and the policy office, was to "assume overview responsibility regarding the handling of a particular case." ERA was to have programmatic responsibility, "including such matters as contract negotiation and administration." These arrangements had been set out in a memorandum from the deputy secretary in July 1978. In fact, what generally occurred was that ERA would write a draft statement and give the General Counsel's Office and the policy office copies. They would then comment on the draft and indicate what changes they thought should be made. This was generally done at the staff level. When the document seemed acceptable to all, staff members would give it to their supervisors with a memo requesting their concurrence.

Despite the seemingly clear definition of responsibilities in this memorandum, the actual process of filing statements had a history of conflict about control over the process and substance of the comments, which resulted in two symptomatic processes. The first was that ERA would send a memo requesting permission to file in a particular proceeding. After the General Counsel's Office and the policy office agreed that DOE should file in this case, ERA would interpret this as permission to file whatever they wrote. Staff people in the policy office had tried to stop this interpretation by not signing the initial memorandum until ERA stated what the substance of the statement would be. ERA said that they needed the signature to justify hiring consultants to do the analysis which would be the basis for what was said. Since they could not justify spending money on an analysis unless they knew that they would be involved in the proceeding, they could not say what the statement would be until after the authorization to file was signed.

The second situation is related to the first. Having convinced ERA that the policy office needed to sign off on the substance of the statement as well as the fact, the policy office would receive a draft of the statement two or three days before the filing date. As with other documents, the policy office responsibility was to make sure that what was said in the document was consistent with DOE policy. Often this was the first time that the department had "said" anything on this specific topic. The document could, however, have implications that were either consistent or inconsistent with related departmental policies. This determination was based on the interpretation of the policy office staff member involved in the process and other relevant members of the policy office. If, as was quite common, the staff member felt that something needed to be changed before the policy office could concur on the statement, the people in ERA would say that they did not have enough time and that they would miss the filing deadline if they had to change.

As discussed in the description of the writing of the National Energy Transportation Study (NETS) in Chapter 4, this office in ERA was particularly mission-oriented. Its members considered themselves to be experts in railroad accounting and finance. They felt strongly that they needed to protect the interest of the coal consumer against the avarice of the railroads. In their eyes, people who opposed their stands either understood railroad accounting and finance but wanted the railroads to make extraordinary profits or simply did not understand the complexities of the field. The Interstate Commerce Commission fell into the first group, the policy office in DOE fell into the second. Thus, when the staff member from the policy office suggested substantive changes in the statements being filed, the reaction from ERA was angry resistance.

Confronting this sort of resistance was considered by people in the policy office to be a normal part of life in DOE. When the policy office staff member related her concern over the reaction of ERA during one filing incident to the deputy assistant secretary of the office, his response was, "If someone hasn't gotten angry with me by the end of the day, I know I haven't been doing my job" (field notes, 7/30/80).

The Office of the General Counsel had always been involved in filing these statements, as specified in the 1978 memorandum. In fact, the statements had to be submitted by a lawyer since they were considered to be legal documents. The major concern of this office, however, was that the document be legally correct. That office had most of the department's legal expertise and was certainly the final arbiter of legal issues. The General Counsel staff member could make a narrow interpretation of that responsibility and approve the document if there were no legal errors. Some General Counsel staff members had taken that position. Just prior to the passage of the Staggers Rail Act, however, there was a change in the General Counsel staff, and a different person became responsible for taking part in this process. This person interpreted the responsibility more broadly, such that the document had to be consistent with positions that her office supported before she would approve it.

This change in the General Counsel staff added to the existing tension in the situation. As the General Counsel staff member began to suggest substantive changes in the ERA statements, conflict arose between her and the ERA staff members. This may have been partially responsible for producing a polarized situation in which the General Counsel and policy staff members worked closely together and the two ERA staff members worked with one another. The fact that the General Counsel and policy offices were in the same building while the ERA office was across town may have contributed to this outcome as well.

The Process

The process for the revenue adequacy rulemaking overlapped with a similar process on a related rulemaking on railroad transportation contracts, which had begun with a publication in the Federal Register October 24, 1980; a statement was filed January 8, 1981. A few days before this proceeding was over, the General Counsel and policy staff members commented to one another on how upsetting it was to think about going into the next "round" with the same people from ERA (field notes, 1/5/81).

On Tuesday, January 6, as the action was drawing to a close on the railroad transportation contracts, the people from the General Counsel and policy offices began to turn their attention to the next proceeding. The General Counsel staff member was primarily interested in starting to learn about the revenue adequacy issue. She proposed talking to someone at the ICC about the proposed regulation. The policy staff member was concerned about getting ERA to produce their statement so that comments could be made on it. She suggested that they set up a meeting with ERA on Friday. That way, they would have some time to find out about the issue and ERA would have time to write a draft statement. This would leave plenty of time for disagreements to be resolved before the filing deadline.

During the last filing the ERA staff members had said they did not want to have anything more to do with the policy staff member. For this reason, both the policy and General Counsel staff members felt that interactions were more likely to be productive if they were initiated by the General Counsel staff member. They felt it would be even more effective to have her boss talk with the ERA staff members' boss. Therefore, she had talked with her boss about setting up a meeting for Friday, but he had said that he wanted to know more about the issue before he did that.

The next day, the General Counsel staff member called ERA to talk about when they would be able to provide the first draft of the statement. One of the staff members from ERA said that he was going to bring it over that afternoon. Later that day, he brought over some handwritten notes on revenue adequacy. The policy and General Counsel staff members read them and penciled in comments; then the General Counsel staff member gave them to her boss to look at.

Meanwhile, the policy office staff member called the ICC and got the name of a person to talk to. She called and set up an appointment with him for 2:30 the next day (Thursday, January 8). Later that day, she read the railroad revenue adequacy Notice of Proposed Rulemaking and started making a list of what parts of it were important to DOE and what should be said about them. These are the first signs of what would later become a completely separate statement by the General Counsel and policy staff members.

At 10:30 Thursday the General Counsel staff member received a draft statement on revenue adequacy from the consultants that ERA had retained for this proceeding. This was not the statement that would be filed with the ICC. As it bore very little resemblance to the handwritten notes received the day before, it was never clear why, or even by whom, this report had been sent. The staff members in ERA were not available that morning to explain, and other events quickly overtook this incident.

That afternoon policy and General Counsel staff members met with the ICC staff to discuss the revenue adequacy proposal and to have him explain what was meant by certain passages in the Notice of Proposed Rulemaking.

When the policy staff member arrived at work Friday, an outline of a proposed statement was on her chair. On it was a note from one of the ERA staff members suggesting a meeting to discuss the statement on Monday, January 12. She called the General Counsel staff member to tell her about this and to see what she had heard from ERA. She had received the same outline with a similar note from the other ERA staff person. That afternoon the General Counsel and policy office staff members gathered more information. One of them reviewed the rule-making while the other reviewed the text of the act.

On Monday, the policy office staff member called the General Counsel staff person to talk about meeting with ERA as suggested on Friday. She said that the ERA staff members had called her to say that they were going to bring a five-page summary argument over by noon the next day. They were no longer interested in meeting that day. In fact, later in the day during a phone call, the policy staff member suggested that the four people working on this get together. The ERA staff member on the other end of the line said that he would rather that policy and the General Counsel's office just phone in their comments.

That same morning the General Counsel staff member continued work from the day before on the rulemaking. The policy staff member called ERA to talk with one of the two people working on this about what the impact of the revenue adequacy proceeding would be, regardless of what standards were used. This question was prompted from reading the act and seeing that revenue adequacy was only mentioned in a few places and it was not clear how critical the standards would be. The need for DOE to file a statement at all was not obvious. The ERA staff responded that they (at ERA) strongly believed it would be very important in maintaining reasonable rates for coal hauling. He said that any fool could see that was true.

The policy and General Counsel staff members met Monday afternoon. They planned to talk with three people to get more information. One was an expert in the field who worked for a Washington law firm. The second was a consultant that the policy staff member had retained to help educate her about the issues involved in the rulemakings. The third person was the staff member at the ICC they had spoken to earlier. In preparation they noted all of the places in the Staggers Rail Act that revenue adequacy made a difference. They also generated a list of questions to ask. These lists represented two aspects of the process that were at issue: whether DOE should file a statement at all in this proceeding and what the statement should say if DOE did file.

Two days later, ERA finally sent the draft statement to the Office of the General Counsel. This was the first time that anyone outside of ERA saw what they proposed to say about the rulemaking. It was January 14, five days before the deadline. The General Counsel staff member called the policy staff member who was at home on sick leave to tell her that the statement had arrived and that she thought it was terrible. They decided that she should contact the consultant the policy staff member had retained and have him look at the draft. The consultant read the draft and also thought it was terrible. Both the consultant and the General Counsel staff member felt that many of the arguments made in the document were wrong and that the positions taken reflected ERA's bias rather than positions of the DOE as a whole. The consultant suggested that he rewrite the statement. The General Counsel staff member called the policy staff member again to discuss the consultant's suggestion. They decided it would be better to have him come in the next morning and talk with them about the issues so that they could either rewrite the statement themselves or tell ERA what they thought needed to be done.

The next day, Thursday, the policy staff member arrived at 8:30 and read the ERA draft from the day before. (ERA had not yet sent this statement to policy; she had obtained a copy from the General Counsel staff member.) The General Counsel and policy staff members met with the consultant from 10:00 to 12:00. Afterwards they talked about rewriting the statement and what needed to be done in the next few days. At 2:00 that afternoon, an ERA staff member called the General Counsel staff member to say that there had, in fact, been an extension of the filing date. Statements were now due on January 23 rather than January 19. She called the policy staff member to tell her the news. They decided to call it quits for the day and to take things up again on the following Monday, January 19.

On Monday the General Counsel and policy staff members took up the problem of what to do with the ERA draft. They drafted and sent (from the Office of the General Counsel) a memo to ERA requesting additional information and clarification of their draft statement.

Two days later, on January 21, the General Counsel staff member received a revision of ERA's earlier draft. That afternoon all four people met to discuss questions posed in the memo sent from the Office of the General Counsel on Monday. This was the first time that the ERA staff members knew that the policy staff member had seen their draft statement. The policy staff member had a prior commitment and had to leave before the meeting adjourned. The meeting was not going well when she left. To the General Counsel and policy staff members, the ERA people seemed to be evading the questions. To the ERA staff members, the General Counsel and policy people seemed to be unable to understand what they were being told. A little later, in partial response to a question posed by the General Counsel staff member, one of the ERA people slammed his fist on the table and called her an idiot. She walked out of the meeting and returned to her office. There she wrote up a separate statement that she proposed filing in this case. The next day General Counsel and policy staff members revised this statement; it was completed at 1:15 and sent to ERA.

After the meeting of the day before, the General Counsel staff member was in no mood to talk with the people in ERA. So later that day, the policy staff member called them to find out when they would have a new draft ready that incorporated the new statement she and the General Counsel staff member had written. The person at ERA said that they were going to go and talk directly with the General Counsel staff member's supervisor to work out some position.

The next day, Friday, was the filing deadline. The policy staff member talked with her supervisor about the draft statement. The day before she had prepared sets of both the proposed drafts for him to read. Her superiors needed to say something very soon if they felt strongly about any particular part of the statement. He said that both drafts seemed similarly obscure in their discussion of accounting, that the issue was relatively unimportant to the main interests of their office, that it was not clear what impact any decision would make in national energy goals, and that given these points, if the three parts of the department engaged in this process could agree on what to say, then the department should not file anything. This meant that no one else in policy would be getting involved, whether to back what the policy staff member wanted or not. It also meant that any currently conceivable resolution of the issue would be acceptable to the policy office.

Later, the General Counsel staff member called the policy staff member to say that the ERA people were coming to her office. Her supervisor had refused to meet with them, so they would be meeting with her to work out some position. She asked that the policy staff member join them. At 11:30 the ERA staff members arrived bringing a new draft of the statement. All four staff members met until 1:45, when they had agreed on a final statement. This statement combined points from each of the proposed drafts; as a result it did not present a clear position. The draft was typed and printed by the policy office support staff and delivered by the General Counsel staff member to the ICC at 5:00.

APPENDIX B

Analysts' Activities During the Observation Period

Gregory's Activities: Methanol

The following list shows the people who are involved in the three-phase study on the production and marketing of methanol that Gregory reported on. Their organizational affiliation is indicated in parentheses; all of the organizations except for the Department of Energy (DOE) are consulting firms.

> Gregory Finn (DOE)
> Marvin Wayne (DOE)
> Ned Nash (HKV)
> V. Howard (HKV)
> Isa French (Isa French Inc.)
> Vernon Gould (Kron)
> Henry Loos (Omnion)
> Nathan Greene (XVA)
> Ted Prine (XVA)

Week 1: December 15–19, 1980

Early in the week, while visiting an office on work unrelated to the methanol study, Gregory noticed a report on methanol that he had not seen before. He passed the report on to HKV.

Thursday: Gregory contacted a person at XVA about another matter. They ended up talking about the methanol study, and it turned out that XVA had just completed a report for the DOE Advanced Technology office that could be helpful to what Gregory was doing, so they set up a meeting to swap information.

Friday: Gregory spent several hours at HKV going over the final run of the Phase I report.

General: Over the week, Gregory talked on the phone with a number of people in order to take care of the preliminaries for a meeting on Saturday. At the meeting they were to discuss finishing up the Phase I report and beginning the Phase II report. The telephone conversations dealt with specific areas of concern. He talked with Vernon Gould (Kron) once a day about the supply side, production costs, and setting up Phase II of the report. He talked with Isa French Monday, Tuesday, and Thursday mornings about the regulatory barrier area and the scope of the Phase II effort he'd be engaged in. He talked with Henry Loos (Omnion) twice about the in-use areas of the Phase I report. He talked with Ned Nash (HKV) twice a day. They discussed the in-use area of Volumes I and II of the Phase I report, what should go in Volume I and II and what stage the production was in. During the week, Gregory also read both the report on methanol that he had passed on to HKV and the Research Guidance Studies produced by Fossil Energy in DOE to assess gasoline from coal by methanol-to-gasoline and SASOL-type Fischer-Tropsch technologies.

Week 2: December 22–26, 1980

Gregory received the copies of the Phase I report. He submitted these to his office director and the deputy assistant secretary. Once they approved the report, Gregory would be able to send the copies out for comment to other people in the department.

Henry Loos and Ned Nash prepared a draft task order for the Phase II work. (HKV was responsible for the task order because it was the consulting firm the DOE had the contract with; Omnion, Kron, and Isa French Inc. were all subcontractors through HKV.) Loos and Nash brought the task order to Gregory's office. Isa French and Vernon Gould joined them there, and the five of them reviewed the task order. They found some errors, corrected them, and gave it to the office director to approve, which he did the next day.

Week 3: December 29, 1980–January 2, 1981

The task order had to be approved next by the technical advisor for the policy office, whose approval was required on all task orders for contracts that go through the policy office. He received the task order on Wednesday, December 31.

The same day Gregory met with Nathan Greene from XVA for an hour to discuss methanol and the applicability of the XVA report to what Gregory was interested in doing. If he could work it out, Gregory wanted to include XVA in the work order. He set up a meeting with HKV and XVA for 2:00 Monday, January 5, to discuss what XVA could contribute.

Week 4: January 5–9, 1981

Monday: The meeting that was set up with XVA fell through, but Gregory met with Ned Nash from HKV who had come for the meeting. They discussed the description of the work they would be doing in the task order (called the "scope of work") and revised it. The technical advisor rejected the task order. He wanted the scope of work to be more simply stated and the statement about funding to be more clear. Gregory made the changes, had the task order retyped, and carried it back to the technical advisor.

Tuesday: Gregory met with Vernon Gould and Isa French about the possibility of including XVA in the study and what it would mean for what they were doing. They concluded that it would have no impact on what French was doing but would have a considerable impact on the work of Gould and Nash of HKV. Gregory had a meeting with Nathan Greene and Ted Prine from XVA to discuss the possibility of working together. Gregory told them what was in the current scope of work. They told him what they had done in the report that they could update for Gregory. Prine said that he would send Gregory the report. Isa French had planned to brief Gregory's office director on what he was going to do for the Phase II report, but this briefing was cancelled.

Wednesday–Thursday: Gregory asked the office administrative assistant to see what was happening with the technical advisor and the task order. He found out that the technical advisor had neither approved nor rejected the order.

Friday: Gregory asked the office director to ask the technical advisor about the task order. Gregory also had a meeting with Nash, Loos, and Greene to discuss the work proposed for XVA to do. XVA submitted a description of the work they proposed to do. Gregory asked them to change it because they were doing all in-use analysis and he wanted them to do some on the supply side as well. They were to call back around noon on Monday.

General: Gregory had reviewed tables of major issues affecting different phases of methanol production and picking areas for further research in Phase II. Three areas that he was particularly interested in were regulatory issues, the trade-off between methanol and M-gas, and an analysis of some blends of methanol and whether or not there are problems with them. He had also been thinking about a build-up scenario for introducing methanol into the infrastructure of the industry. The current situation was that the auto industry wanted assured supplies of methanol before it would develop cars that used it and the methanol industry wanted assured production of autos before it would make that much methanol.

Week 5: January 12–16, 1981

Monday: Gregory discussed the Phase II work with people from XVA and HKV. The technical advisor cleared the HKV task order after the office director asked him to look at it. It had to be approved next by the DOE procurement office. Gregory hand carried an advance copy to this office and discussed it with the person who will have to approve it.

Tuesday: Gregory worked up a rough draft for a task order for the work XVA will be doing.

Wednesday: The administrative assistant hand carried a formal copy of the HKV task order (advance copy sent on Monday) to the DOE procurement office. Gregory held a meeting with people from XVA and HKV to finalize the draft of the XVA task order.

Friday: Gregory called the DOE procurement officer to check on the HKV task order. The procurement officer had forgotten about it but thought that it had probably been sent to the contract officer in the policy office. This would be standard procedure.

General: Gregory distributed the Phase I drafts this week for comments from a number of people representing different parts of the Department of Energy: two people from Resource Applications, one from Conservation and Solar, one from Fossil Energy, and four in the policy office. The person from Fossil Energy and one of the people from the policy office were in fact no longer employed by the department, but Gregory asked for their comments because until recently they had been working in the department on methanol-related issues, and they knew a lot about the area.

XVA brought Gregory a copy of the report that they were going to update for him. He gave it to the office director to read. Gregory expected some flak this week from the Advanced Technology office in DOE about using XVA. The XVA report had been written under contract with Advanced Technology. Since XVA was still under contract with them, the work XVA would do to revise the report for Gregory would be paid for by them. The rule that produced this result helped ensure that DOE did not pay twice for the same work, but it could also produce tension between offices within DOE. Advanced Technology did call XVA, but that was all. Gregory had three phone calls from Isa French and one with Vernon Gould in which they discussed the work that XVA was going to do for the Phase II report. They talked about swapping tasks so as to make the best use of everyone.

Gregory had been doing some reading on what areas he wanted to concentrate on for the Phase II report. Some money was freed up by including XVA in Phase II, partly because they could use Advanced Technology's contract to pay XVA and partly because XVA only had to update the work they had already done, whereas Gregory had projected having to pay for all of the work. Gregory felt that the regulatory area would be the most fruitful to explore. There were also two areas that he could either make issues out of or make recommendations to Fossil Energy (FE) about: safety in handling materials and the possibility of reducing costs in technical areas.

Week 6: *January 19–23, 1981*

Monday: Gregory called the DOE procurement officer again about the HKV task order. It turned out that it had not been sent to the contract officer in the policy office as he had been told the week before. Gregory spent much of the day talking with the procurement officer about the task order and an option for a second year on the contract. The procurement officer signed the task order and the second-year option by the end of the day.

Isa French came in to give the office director the briefing that had been postponed from the week before on his Phase II efforts. He talked about the problems caused by regulations and what might be done about them. Most of his efforts in Phase II would be on identifying which regulations had enough impact that DOE should try to do something about them.

Wednesday: Gregory notified all parties involved that the HKV task order had been signed (Nash, Gould, French, Loos).

Wednesday–Thursday: Gregory spent some time getting the XVA task order approved by people in the policy office. This involved talking with the technical advisor and the contract officer about it.

Friday: Gregory hand carried the XVA task order to the DOE procurement officer, who signed it. Gregory called XVA to tell them that it had gone through.

General: Gregory made several calls to the people involved in the report about a meeting the next Tuesday (January 27). They were to meet with the office director to brief him on the Phase II work plan. The briefing was to include the "nitty-gritty" scope of effort—details of the content of the studies.

Week 7: *January 26–30, 1981*

Monday: Gregory prepared for briefing the office director the next day. Early in the morning, he talked on the phone with French, Nash, Gould, and Prine about the briefing and what would be expected of them there. Then there was a meeting at HKV from 9:00 to 3:00. Gregory and Marvin Wayne were there from the policy office in DOE. Howard and Nash were there from HKV. Gould (Kron), Loos (Omnion), and French

(French, Inc.) were also present. They developed a document to use for the briefing.

Tuesday: Gould, Nash, and French each called in the morning to talk about "the pitch" for the office director's briefing. They had done some "fine tuning" of their individual areas after the meeting ended on Monday. The meeting to brief the office director took one hour. The same people who were at the Monday meeting were there, except that there was one more person from XVA and French was not there. The office director asked that, prior to doing what they planned to do, they sort out the final cost to the consumer of methanol vs. M-gas. This was not easy to do since the costs of retrofit and other factors would need to be calculated. After the meeting, Gregory asked everyone to give him detailed work plans for the work requested by the office director by the following Wednesday.

Nash (HKV) and Gregory discussed the fact that the first scope of work (approved in week 6) had the tasks in it that XVA is now going to do. They have added some tasks to the HKV task order to use up the money that was freed by removing the tasks that XVA is doing. This new task order now has to be approved.

Wednesday: Gregory talked with Isa French about a meeting the following Monday and about the work plans. He talked with Nash and asked him to determine which of the assignments in the new task order were over and above the original tasks. He and Gould had a general philosophical discussion on the methanol work effort.

Thursday: Gregory drafted a letter and scope-of-work revision for the HKV task order. He hand carried it to a person in the DOE procurement office and got his comments on it. Then he made some minor administrative changes and took it back to the DOE procurement office for more comments.

Friday: Gregory formulated a final version of the letter and the task order for the procurement office. He had the office director read the rough draft to make sure that he had no objections. Gregory carried it over to the DOE procurement office in the afternoon.

Week 8: February 2-6, 1981

Monday: Gregory talked on the phone with Nash, Gould, and French, concerning the new work plans for the Phase II report. They talked about how the five contractor groups were working together and how to coordinate their efforts. Later that day, all five contractors had an "integration meeting" on the work plans. The procurement office in DOE approved the revised task order. A person from the Office of Technology Assessment (OTA) called to ask if he could get a copy of the Phase I report. Gregory asked the office director, who said it was all right. He sent the Phase I report, and OTA sent over some documents concerning energy from biological processes (e.g., methanol from wood scraps).

Tuesday: Gregory talked on the phone with Nash, Gould, and French. The conversations were principally questions and requests for clarification resulting from the meeting the day before.

Wednesday: Gregory talked with a person from Alcohol Week about the Phase I report. They talked about what should and should not be put in an article about it. Marvin was present as a witness.

Thursday: Gregory had not yet received the work plans from Omnion and HKV. He had requested the week before that they be given to him by Wednesday. He called the contracting officer and told him to "stop work" from Omnion and HKV until Gregory got their work plans. Gregory spent some time reading some of the OTA documents regarding energy from biological processes.

Friday: The work plan for the group was hand delivered to Gregory. Gregory called the DOE contract officer to let him know that he had received the work plans. Gregory met with Gould about the work plan from HKV. After looking at the draft, Gregory felt that it was still incomplete. They talked about the need to pin down the "deliverables" in order to finalize the plan. ("Deliverables" are the product of a contract, what the contractor is to deliver to the person or organization contracting for the work.)

Gregory called Isa French to see if he had gotten the contractual "turn-on" from HKV. (Isa was a subcontractor.) He had not. Gregory called HKV and talked with Howard who said that the letter had been sent out (to Isa) on Wednesday and that he would make sure that Isa got the letter.

Gregory spent some more time reading the OTA documents.

Week 9: February 9–13, 1981

Tuesday: Gregory and Marvin met with people from XVA. They discussed the choice of a region to study. XVA was leaning heavily toward using California. Gregory, however, thought that California was not representative, that there was too much gas for methanol available there.

Thursday: Gregory had set up a meeting between XVA and HKV for today. They met and discussed regions to study.

Week 10: February 16–20, 1981

Tuesday: Gregory called everyone except Omnion to see what was going on. Everything was moving along as planned. In making these calls, Gregory also set up a meeting for Wednesday to discuss regions.

Wednesday: Gregory and the office director met with Nash and

Howard from HKV to talk about regions. They chose the Illinois region, primarily because it seemed representative: coal is available, also water, land, and pipeline transport. In addition, choosing this region would fit in with a national strategy for dealing with problems in more than one region since using methanol locally would free up natural gas and gasoline coming from the Gulf of Mexico to go to the Northeast region. They also discussed the marketing study section (methanol beyond the plant gate). Gregory thought that they might have short-changed that area. They discussed some possibilities but left it up to HKV to come up with a proposal. Gregory suggested getting some expertise (perhaps from Isa French or someone like him) to help out, or they could get another consultant. Gregory wanted some assurances that there was someone in there who knew what she or he was doing.

Thursday: Gregory spoke with Howard (HKV) and French on the phone. Both calls were about routine things, exchange of information (e.g., name of book, person to call). They set up a meeting for next Wednesday. This would be the first meeting on where things stand (status review meeting). The group planned to have these meetings about every three weeks.

Friday: Gregory talked with Gould about overall coordination. Gregory said that he was pretty happy with the way things stood. Gregory talked with Isa French to tell him that the status review meeting on Wednesday would be at HKV.

General: Gregory had received comments back on the Phase I report from everyone he sent it to (see week 5) except the two people who were no longer working for the department. The one who had worked in PE called this week to tell him that he had finished Volume I and would call with comments early next week. Gregory had received a lot of calls from around the country requesting copies of the Phase I report, which would have to be approved by the department before it could be sent out. Gregory would use the comments he had just received to revise the report so it could be approved and sent out to the people requesting it.

Week 11: February 23–27, 1981

Monday–Tuesday: On both days Gregory talked with French, Gould, and Howard about the status review coming up on Wednesday.

Wednesday: The first status review meeting was held at HKV. It lasted four hours. French, Nash, Howard, Gould, and Loos attended along with Gregory and Marvin from DOE. Late in the afternoon Gregory received fact sheets about the contract from OMB, which he had to fill in.

Thursday: Gregory talked with Gould, French, Howard, and Loos by phone about the meeting the day before. All of these people saw the regulatory analysis as a key area. Gould and French both said that a full analysis in the regulatory area could be done only for transportation issues, because of lack of funds. Gregory filled out the OMB fact sheets he had received the day before. In doing so, he talked with Howard (HKV), Gould (Kron), a person from Omnion, and a person from XVA. He turned the fact sheets in at the end of the day.

Week 12: March 2–6, 1981

A new office director was announced this week.

Thursday: French came in to discuss regulatory assessment in the morning. Gregory asked him for a detailed cost estimate for areas other than transportation including utilities, industrial, commercial, and residential. Gregory talked with Gould about studying utilities and the need for a detailed assessment of the regulatory area to determine potential cost impacts. Gould agreed that such an assessment would be important.

General: Gregory and Marvin discussed the current work plan during the week. Gregory had no specific comments. He decided not to change anything until he could talk with the new office director. Gregory planned to get him up to speed and then see if he wanted any changes. Marvin and Gregory also reviewed and commented on a comparison of M-gas and neat methanol that the old office director wanted them to look at to decide if there was enough difference between the two fuels to proceed with the methanol study. Gregory received the Liquefaction Technology Assessment Phase I report, produced by Oak Ridge National Laboratory on contract with Fossil Energy in DOE. He did not read it.

Marvin's Activities: Liquefaction and Gasification

During the observation period, Marvin reported on several activities. He was involved in the methanol report with Gregory; he also worked on a contribution to the policy office's annual Policy Planning and Fiscal Guidance Report and spent much of his time reviewing unsolicited proposals and keeping current on his issues.

Week 1: December 15–19, 1980

Policy Planning and Fiscal Guidance Report: Marvin had submitted an issue paper on liquefaction and gasification on December 12. Most of the paper had been written ten days earlier as a special report to a group making preliminary policy decisions for the new administration. At the beginning of week 1 the paper was reformulated as an issue paper for the Policy Planning and Fiscal Guidance exercise. The paper dealt with the issue of whether the government should build liquefaction and gasification plants. In the past, there was not the economic justification to interest the private sector in building these plants; as a result, the government built them. Fossil Energy (FE) in DOE had been largely responsible for the programs that have built these plants. It was now being suggested that a less costly alternative would be to build demonstration plants large enough to show that a commercial-scale plant is possible without building a full-scale plant. In his issue paper Marvin argued that this alternative would be less expensive and equally effective. There were some political implications of this proposal that Marvin was aware of but did not discuss in the paper. He thought the proposal would "emasculate" the FE program by drastically reducing the budget. It would also take away pet political projects established in certain states.

General: During the week, Marvin read an analysis of Canadian natural gas. He talked with a person in the Conservation and Solar office of Policy about the availability and cost of diesel fuel. He also talked with the Southwest Research Institute about doing research on methanol as a fuel and the corrosiveness of methanol.

Week 2: December 22–26, 1980

Marvin on vacation.

Week 3: December 29, 1980–January 2, 1981

Marvin in the hospital for scheduled operation.

Week 4: January 5–9, 1981

Marvin in the hospital.

Week 5: January 12–16, 1981

Marvin recovering at home.

Week 6: January 19–23, 1981

Marvin returned to work at the end of the week. No relevant work to report.

Week 7: January 26–30, 1981

Marvin spent much of the week catching up on reading, in which he found several relevant items. Shell Coppers was considering setting up an office to sell gasifiers. This would greatly enhance synfuel development, which assumes the availability of gasifiers. General Motors had stated that electric motors were a rip-off. A methanol-using engine was the main nonpolluting alternative. To Marvin's knowledge, no one had looked at the comparisons of other motors with electric, which he attributed to "the politics of [GM's] being #1 and the visibility of that position to the hill [Congress]." Marvin thought the new administration might agree with General Motors and change the current favored status of the electric motor, which might increase the likelihood of more research on methanol-using engines. A report on the international liquid natural gas (LNG) trade dealt with questions of the most efficient way to import natural gas and the effect of these imports on markets for domestic liquid natural gas and methanol.

Marvin learned that the synfuels program had been cut by OMB this week. This would have an indirect effect on his work, though it was not clear what the effect would be.

Week 8: February 2–6, 1981

Methanol report: Marvin talked with Gregory's contractors three times this week about problems with the methanol report, especially the review of the existing methanol marketplace and existing capacity.

General: Marvin called the authors of a report comparing international trade issues for methanol and LNG. They talked for a couple of hours about the assumptions in the report. The main issue was what to do with the natural gas that comes up with oil. It was usually wasted, since the currently available alternatives were expensive.

Week 9: February 9–13, 1981

Methanol report: Marvin spent some time investigating an issue in Gregory's methanol report, the economics of moving from crude oil to the refined product used in the gas pump. He found that DOE had very little information on this subject. Within DOE he talked with the Energy Information Administration and the Economic Regulatory Administration. He also called the American Petroleum Institute, AMOCO, TRW, and the Office of Technology Assessment about how the costs might break down. He found that none of them had much information about this.

Marvin started working on updating crude oil price assumptions, an exercise he first did in May 1977. He was updating the information for use in Gregory's methanol report. Gregory's contractors have been using figures that someone in Fossil Energy (DOE) had a contractor produce four years ago, and Marvin thought the report would be better if new numbers were used.

General: Marvin was reviewing an unsolicited proposal for Fossil Energy, submitted by Gulf Oil. It suggested a study comparing production costs of methanol and LNG. Marvin made some calls to see if anyone had information on this topic. He found out that Continental Oil had been doing work on it but was not ready to release anything yet. He also found out something about the state and federal reactions to an excise tax on methanol and received the final report "Fuel Alcohol: An Energy Alternative for the 1980's" by the U.S. National Alcohol Fuels Commission.

Week 10: February 16–20, 1981

No relevant work to report.

Week 11: February 23–27, 1981

Methanol report: This week Marvin finished the preliminary work on crude oil price assumptions. He talked with someone at American Oil to see how they set price estimates and whether they thought his numbers were reasonable. He also called Chase Manhattan for the same reasons; the person he needed to talk to there was not in but would get back to him. Marvin also planned to ask the Economic Regulatory Administration (DOE), the Office of Technology Assessment, and the American Petroleum Institute to review the numbers and comment. He gave the updated numbers to the office director to be released for internal DOE use. In particular, he hoped the figures would be used in Gregory's methanol report.

General: Marvin reviewed an unsolicited proposal from Gulf Oil to look at the economics of recovery of remote natural gas. He commented on the study and suggested expanding it, then sent the proposal back to Fossil Energy.

Week 12: March 2–6, 1981

Methanol report: Marvin spent two days reviewing the work plan for the methanol report for Gregory.

General: Fossil Energy sent Marvin another unsolicited proposal to review; this one concerned different ways to market natural gas. This was a study that Marvin had wanted to have done for a long time and that Fossil Energy was now going to sponsor. He reviewed the proposal and sent back his comments.

Anne's Activities: Impact Assistance

Week 1: December 15–19, 1980

Anne submitted a Policy Planning and Fiscal Guidance issue paper supporting a program on impact assistance and suggesting that the policy office take an active role in such a program. There were currently two impact assistance programs involving the Department of Energy. The larger program was established in Section 601 of the Powerplant and Industrial Fuel Use Act (PIFUA) and was administered jointly by the Department of Energy (DOE) and the Department of Agriculture (DOA). Conservation and Solar within DOE had a $1 million budget to designate states for qualification by demographic characteristics. The Federal Housing Authority (FHA) in DOA then used this list of states to give out the $19 million in impact assistance. The smaller program was run out of the Office of Oil Shale Development in Resource Application with a budget of $2 million this year. Anne was aware that the Office of Management and Budget (OMB) opposed this smaller program because it did not like individual programs. The policy office was currently not involved in either of these programs, and in her issue paper Anne suggested that it should be.

Ilsa Long, the special assistant to the head of Resource Applications, convened a meeting of people from Resource Applications and Conservation and Solar on December 15 to discuss making a proposal from the administration and submitting it to Congress. She had suggested in a memo about a month before that Resource Applications take over the function that Conservation and Solar now had in the PIFUA program. Anne suspected that this was the proposal discussed at the meeting but did not know for sure because the policy office (Anne) was not invited to the meeting.

Week 2: December 22–26, 1980

No relevant work to report.

Week 3: December 29, 1980–January 2, 1981

Anne on vacation.

Week 4: January 5–9, 1981

Anne on vacation.

Week 5: January 12–16, 1981

Anne returned from her vacation on January 16. She called Ilsa Long and learned that the department, through Resource Applications, had $5 million for impact assistance to be allocated on a project-by-project basis. The money was made available by the Defense Production Act and was being used for synfuel production projects. Long was working on legislation and had drafted a bill similar to one already introduced by a senator. Long's proposal differed in that it stipulated that the Department of Energy would run the program rather than the Department of Agriculture and that the Department of Energy would provide loans or loan guarantees rather than grants. (Anne suspected that there were other differences as well, but she had not yet seen the draft.) In the same conversation Long related several pieces of impact assistance news. She talked about having an Office of Impact Assistance under the new Secretary. She also said that a person at OMB was talking about having an interagency task force on impact assistance. Finally, she told Anne about a listing of impact studies that the technical information center had and that her office had expanded and cross-referenced by state. The listing was a guide both to studies and to grant programs.

Week 6: January 19–23, 1981

No relevant work to report.

Week 7: January 26–30, 1981

No relevant work to report.

Week 8: February 2–6, 1981

No relevant work to report.

Week 9: February 9–13, 1981

No relevant work to report.

Week 10: February 16–20, 1981

No relevant work to report.

Week 11: February 23–27, 1981

No relevant work to report.

Week 12: March 2–6, 1981

This week Anne learned of actions taken by the new administration concerning impact assistance, from which she concluded that impact assistance was not seen as an important issue. The budget for fiscal year 1981 (FY81) for the impact assistance program was reduced, from $62 million under Carter to $10 million under Reagan. (Of the $62 million, $20 million went for energy-related projects; see week 1.) The budget for the program was "zeroed out" for FY82. Also, the oil shale program in Resource Applications was to be "zeroed out" or seriously reduced. Another action taken by the new administration would have an indirect effect on impact assistance in the Department of Energy: all people hired under Schedule C were to be fired (these people are not career civil servants). Ilsa Long was among them.

Edna's Activities: Socioeconomic Impacts of Synfuel Production

Week 1: December 15–19, 1980

Case study project: Edna was interested in pushing forward plans for industrial development of synfuels by doing a case study of successes and failures in socioeconomic development relating to industrial development and by establishing guidelines for processes that work on the basis of this case study. Edna was trying to get funding for this project from Resource Applications, but in order to do so she had to convince the deputy assistant secretary of that part of the department. He was then in charge of the task force reviewing synfuels solicitations, or bids for contracts from the department for research and development of synthetic fuels. Reviewing them would take a great deal of time, and there were deadlines that had to be met. Consequently, he was going to be very hard to reach. Edna spent four hours one day talking with the consultant that she wanted to have write the report. She spent another four hours another day talking with a person in Resource Applications about funding for the project.

Week 2: December 22–26, 1980

No relevant work to report.

Week 3: December 29, 1980–January 2, 1981

No relevant work to report.

Week 4: January 5–9, 1981

Edna talked with some people in the environmental section of the department about the socioeconomic impacts of synfuel development. They discussed the DOE history of dealing with socioeconomic legislation and legislation that had not passed. They also talked about the "601 Program" (see Anne's activities, week 1), which gives out money for the socioeconomic impacts of energy development, and DOE's involvement in that program.

Week 5: January 12–16, 1981

Monday, Edna went to a Socioeconomic Committee meeting that lasted half the day. This committee is an internal DOE Committee with members from Conservation and Solar, Environment, Resource Applications, and the policy office. They discussed the governor's stances on socioeconomic development and the possible bottlenecks relating to synfuel development.

Later in the week she went to talk with some people at the *National Geographic*. They had published a special energy issue with a section on socioeconomic impacts. Edna felt that the article presented only the bad side. She made the case that there are positive socioeconomic impacts of energy development as well.

Case study project: She talked with an upper-level official at the Synfuel Corporation about supporting her project.

Week 6: January 19–23, 1981

Edna wrote a "statement of problems" paper for the Socioeconomic Committee meeting held on Tuesday, January 20, which she attended. She also went to a meeting at the Department of Housing and Urban Development concerning socioeconomic problems on Tuesday.

Week 7: January 26–30, 1981

No relevant work to report.

Week 8: February 2–6, 1981

No relevant work to report.

Week 9: February 9–13, 1981

No relevant work to report.

Week 10: February 16–20, 1981

Edna sent a memo to the Assistant General Counsel for Legislation in DOE about the Defense Economic Adjustment Act. This act was to be considered by Congress sometime in the current session. Edna suggested it be revised to take into account "energy-impacted" areas as well as "defense-impacted" areas. She sent copies of the memo to a staff member in Environment and another in Conservation and Solar.

Week 11: February 23–27, 1981

On Friday Edna attended a one-hour meeting of the subcommittee on future actions for the Social Science group of the Socioeconomic Committee. This was the first meeting of this group since January 20. They discussed the potential DOE position on socioeconomic impacts. They also discussed how changes in the budget made by the new administration would influence what the department could do. Responsibility for writing a paper about the proper role for the federal government and the DOE was assigned to the staff person from Conservation and Solar, the same person to whom Edna sent a copy of her memo in week 10. The staff person from Environment who received the memo was also in attendance.

Week 12: March 2–6, 1981

Edna was detailed to the task force which was reviewing synfuel solicitations (see week 1).

Daniel's Activities: Coal Leasing

Daniel's activities in connection with coal leasing included reviewing the status of coal leasing regulations and sales, working on a paper for the Policy Planning and Fiscal Guidance Report, reviewing a coal policy study and a coal competition study that were part of the annual report to Congress from the Energy Information Administration, and commenting on reports on coal leasing and production goals.

Week 1: December 15–19, 1980

Coal leasing regulations and sales: The previous week, the policy office had concurred on the coal lease bidding regulation that would govern the first sale of Western coal lands in ten years. This sale was to occur on January 14, 1981. Resource Applications had the lead on this issue, and Daniel had been involved in reviewing and commenting on the regulations as they had developed over the past thirteen months.

Policy Planning and Fiscal Guidance Report: Daniel was writing a paper on coal leasing for the Policy Planning and Fiscal Guidance Report. He had written the first version of his paper in early November, and this week he revised it for the second time. He went over it with his supervisor and then sent it to the assistant secretary for Policy and Evaluation. (Papers were circulated for approval first within the policy office and then to other offices in the department.)

Annual report to Congress from the Energy Information Administration: Daniel read, reviewed, and commented on the leasing sections in two parts of the annual report from EIA to Congress, the Coal Policy Study and the Coal Competition Study. Daniel questioned certain assumptions about the inflation rate in the Coal Competition Study, which he felt made the estimate of the demand for coal incorrect. He sent his comments back to the EIA offices where the reports were written.

Week 2: December 22–26, 1980

Coal leasing goals: Resource Applications was responsible for producing leasing goals to guide leasing policy. As with the leasing regulations, these goals had to be approved by the assistant secretary of Policy and Evaluation as well as by other parts of the department. Daniel, in general, was responsible for reviewing the goals to make sure that it was appropriate for the policy office to approve them. This review included checking the assumptions and analysis as well as the overall policy statement made.

Daniel had problems of a different nature with this particular report. For no known reason it had sometimes been routed to Daniel and other times to a person in another part of the policy office. The report had first come out in April 1980 and had gone to the other staff member, who had commented on it and sent it back. When the report was revised and sent out for comment again in September, it came to Daniel, who realized from references to earlier comments that this was not a first draft. Daniel called Resource Applications and found out who had made the earlier comments for policy. Daniel called that staff member, and they coordinated their responses to the September version of the report. The latest version had been sent neither to Daniel nor to the other staff member, but to the assistant secretary's office. Daniel learned of this and called the assistant secretary's office to request that it be sent to him. He and the other policy staff member again coordinated their comments.

There were also two substantive problems with this report. First, the 1980 Energy Information Administration forecasts were smaller by about 25 percent than what Resource Applications used in this report; second, the report made a bad case for overleasing though Daniel thought it could make a good case for underleasing.

Week 3: December 29, 1980–January 2, 1981

Daniel on vacation.

Week 4: January 5–9, 1981

Coal production goals: Resource Applications was also responsible for producing coal production goals, to be updated every two years. The numbers were used by the Department of Interior (DOI) for coal leasing management in the Federal Coal Management Program. In fact, the 1978 figures were being used for the upcoming leasing sales (see week 1).

The final report of the 1980 production goals came out of Resource Applications this week. Though earlier versions had been circulated in the policy office, Daniel had not seen them, because the responsibility had belonged to another person in Daniel's office; she had since left the office to work for another part of the Department of Energy. Daniel found he had some real disagreements with the assumptions used in the model that generated the goals which he certainly would have raised if he had seen the report when it first came out. At this point, however, the time for comments was past, and he did not feel that it would be appropriate for him to recommend not concurring. As he said, "To not concur for theoretical reasons does not cut ice with my superiors. This is a pragmatic office, and we work with the best we have. Not concurring on purely theoretical grounds is not an alternative. Shortstopping a process on purely theoretical grounds is against the department's objectives." So Daniel wrote a memorandum to the Assistant Secretary of the policy office recommending concurrence. He also wrote a letter from the assistant secretary of the policy office to the assistant secretary of Resource Applications stating the policy office's concurrence.

Week 5: January 12–16, 1981

Policy Planning and Fiscal Guidance Report: Daniel's superior received comments from Resource Applications on the leasing issue paper that Daniel had written (see week 1) and passed them on to Daniel. There were two major policy issues in the paper. One is the question of how much coal to lease. Resource Applications agreed with policy and the rest of the department that more coal should be leased. The other question was what role the department should have in the leasing process. Resource Applications would like the issue paper to push harder for legislation that would locate the final responsibility for setting leasing goals in the Department of Energy rather than in the Department of Interior. The policy office is taking the position that this should be decided by negotiation between the department secretaries rather than by legislation.

Coal production goals: The policy office gave formal concurrence on the production goals paper. It arrived at Resource Applications on Thursday.

Coal leasing regulations and sales: The planned lease sale took place successfully and satisfactorily on January 14 (see week 1). Three tracts had two bidders each, and some tracts had as many as four bidders. The minimum bid was $25 per acre. In all, seven tracts were auctioned with a price range of from $30 to $500 per acre. Daniel learned that there were a couple of lawsuits pending concerning future leasing regulations. The suits were brought against the Department of Agriculture and the Department of Energy. As a result, the leasing office of the department would have to provide new bidding regulations for the scrutiny of the court by March 15, 1981.

Week 6: January 19–23, 1981

No relevant work to report.

Week 7: January 26–30, 1981

Coal leasing regulations and sales: Daniel learned from the *Energy Daily* the exact terms and quantities of the leases sold on January 14.

Week 8: February 2–6, 1981

No relevant work to report.

Week 9: February 9–13, 1981

No relevant work to report.

Week 10: February 16–20, 1981

Coal production goals: On Wednesday, February 18, Daniel heard that release of the coal production goals paper (see weeks 4 and 5) had been stopped until further notice; the special assistant to the Secretary of Energy had stopped release because the paper had "too many policy content implications." Until this report was approved by everyone, the Department of Interior would continue to use the old figures for production goals. Two sales were scheduled for March and early April and might take place before the report was released.

Week 11: February 23–27, 1981

This week, the leasing office was moved from Resource Applications to Fossil Energy. The individuals in the office would have preferred to be absorbed by the policy office if they could not remain independent. It was rumored that the office would move again within the next eighteen months, from the Department of Energy to the Department of Interior.

Daniel saw a list of issues on a desk in the front office; it had leasing underlined as first and coal exports second. From this Daniel surmised that leasing, as an issue, was getting a high priority. Consequently, he expected to hear from the head of Fossil Energy (new home of the leasing office) and the technical advisor of the policy office, asking what he had done recently. They would particularly want to know about the coal leasing paper for Policy Planning and Fiscal Guidance (see weeks 1 and 5).

Coal Leasing Regulations and Sales: The *Coal Daily* reported that Secretary James Watt (DOI) announced his intention to accelerate the coal leasing schedule and expand the total amount of acreage leased. By wondering why Watt was talking about acreage rather than tons of coal, Daniel gave his opinion that the real coal expertise does not lie in the Department of Interior.

Week 12: March 2–6, 1981

No relevant work to report.

Interview Schedule

1. Education:
2. Position:
3. How long have you been at DOE?
4. How long have you been in your present position?
5. What were you doing before you came to DOE?
6. Prior experience in energy?
7. Why did you come to work for DOE?
8. How would you say you spend most of your time at work?
9. How would you describe DOE's mission?
10. Has DOE's mission changed in the last year?
11. If so (DOE's mission has changed in the last year), how?
12. How would you describe the function of your office?
13. Has the function of your office changed in the last year?
14. If so (the function of your office has changed in the last year), in what ways?
15. What are your responsibilities?
16. Have your responsibilities changed in the last year?
17. If so (your responsibilities have changed in the last year), what were they before they changed?
18. Who do you work with in fulfilling your responsibilities?
19. How much of the work that you do in an average week is represented in your office's weekly activities report?
20. What percentage of the deadlines you receive on assignments are 24 hours or less?
21. What percentage of the deadlines you receive on assignments are 24 to 48 hours?

22. What percentage of the deadlines you receive on assignments are 48 hours to a week?

23. What percentage of the deadlines you receive on assignments are more than one week?

24. Who are the people you talk with most frequently over the course of the work day?

25. If you had been ill yesterday, would you have been concerned about missing anything or about not being able to do something?

26. What that you did yesterday would have been done by someone else (if you had been ill)?

27. When you called in sick, would you have given any messages besides that you could not come in?

28. Who would you have called or wanted to speak with?

29. Are there any other calls you would have made?

30. Why do you continue to work for DOE?

31. Tell me a story about the department or give me a metaphor of the department. (Note: only around half of the interviews included the "give me a metaphor of the department" phrase.)

Reference Matter

Bibliography

Allison, Graham T. 1971. *The Essence of Decision: Explaining the Cuban Missile Crisis*. Boston: Little, Brown.

Atkinson, Joseph D., and Jay M. Shafritz. 1985. *The Real Stuff: A History of NASA's Astronaut Recruitment Program*. New York: Praeger.

Baier, Vicki Eaton, James G. March, and Harold Saetren. 1986. "Implementation and Ambiguity." *Scandinavian Journal of Management Studies* 2: 197–212.

Bateson, Gregory. 1972. *Steps to an Ecology of Mind*. New York: Ballantine Books.

Benveniste, Guy. 1972. *The Politics of Expertise*. Berkeley, Calif.: Glendessary Press.

Berger, Seymour M., and William Lambert. 1968. "Stimulus-Response Theory in Contemporary Social Psychology." In Gardner Lindzey and Elliot Aronson, eds. *The Handbook of Social Psychology*, Vol. 1. Reading, Mass.: Addison-Wesley.

Blau, Peter M. 1968. "The Hierarchy of Authority in Organization." *American Journal of Sociology* 73: 453–67 (Jan.).

Blumer, Herbert. 1969. *Symbolic Interactionism: Perspective and Method*. Englewood Cliffs, N.J.: Prentice Hall.

Bozeman, Barry. 1986. "The Credibility of Policy Analysis: Between Method and Use." *Policy Studies Journal* 14(4): 519–39.

Brunsson, Nils. 1985. *The Irrational Organization*. New York: Wiley.

Cicourel, Aaron V. 1968. *The Social Organization of Juvenile Justice*. New York: Wiley.

Cohen, Michael D. 1985. "Stability and Change in Systems of Standard Operating Procedures." Paper presented at Stanford Workshop on Political-Military Decision Making, Mar. 1985.

Cohen, M. D., and J. G. March. 1974. *Leadership and Ambiguity: The American College President*. New York: McGraw-Hill.

Cohen, M. D., J. G. March, and J. P. Olsen. 1972. "A Garbage Can

Model of Organizational Choice." *Administrative Science Quarterly* 17: 1–25.

Crozier, Michel. 1964. *The Bureaucratic Phenomenon.* Chicago: University of Chicago Press.

Cyert, Richard M., and J. G. March. 1963. *Behavioral Theory of the Firm.* Englewood Cliffs, N.J.: Prentice Hall.

Dahl, Robert A. 1961. *Who Governs.* New Haven: Yale University Press.

———. 1963. *Modern Political Analysis.* Englewood Cliffs, N.J.: Prentice Hall.

Derthick, Martha. 1972. *New Towns in Town.* Washington, D.C.: Urban Institute.

Derthick, Martha, and Paul J. Quirk. 1985. *The Politics of Deregulation.* Washington, D.C.: Brookings Institution.

Downs, Anthony. 1957. *An Economic Theory of Democracy.* New York: Harper & Row.

Dryzek, John. 1982. "Policy Analysis as a Hermeneutic Activity." *Policy Sciences* 14: 309–29.

Dyson, Freeman. 1979. *Disturbing the Universe.* New York: Harper & Row.

Eckstein, Harry. 1975. "Case Study and Theory in Political Science." In F. I. Greenstein and N. W. Polsby, eds. *Handbook of Political Science,* Vol. 7. Reading, Mass.: Addison-Wesley.

Edelman, Murray. 1964. *The Symbolic Uses of Politics.* Chicago: University of Illinois Press.

———. 1977. *Political Language: Words That Succeed and Policies That Fail.* New York: Academic Press.

Elster, Jon. 1983. *Sour Grapes: Studies in the Subversion of Rationality.* New York: Cambridge University Press.

Feldman, Martha S., and J. G. March. 1981. "Information in Organizations as Signal and Symbol." *Administrative Science Quarterly* 26: 171–86.

Fritschler, A. Lee. 1983. *Smoking and Politics: Policy Making and the Federal Bureaucracy,* 3d ed. Englewood Cliffs, N.J.: Prentice Hall.

Geertz, Clifford. 1973. *The Interpretation of Cultures.* New York: Basic Books.

George, Alexander L. 1982. "Case Studies and Theory Development." Paper presented to the Second Annual Symposium on Information Processing in Organizations. Carnegie-Mellon University, Oct. 15–16, 1982.

Goffman, Erving. 1974. *Frame Analysis: An Essay on the Organization of Experience.* New York: Harper & Row.

———. 1983. *Forms of Talk.* Philadelphia: University of Pennsylvania Press.

Goodman, Nelson. 1978. *Ways of Worldmaking*. Indianapolis, Ind.: Herbett Publishing Co.

Goodwin, Craufurd D., ed. 1981. *Energy Policy in Perspective*. Washington, D.C.: Brookings Institution.

Gouldner, A. W. 1954. *Patterns of Industrial Bureaucracy*. Glencoe, Ill.: Free Press.

Gramlich, Edward M. 1981. *Benefit-Cost Analysis of Government Programs*. Englewood Cliffs, N.J.: Prentice Hall.

Gregory, R. J. 1982. "Understanding Public Bureaucracy." *Public Sector* 4(2/3) : 3–12.

Gulick, L. H., and L. Urwick. 1937. *Papers on the Science of Administration*. New York: Institute of Public Administration, Columbia University.

Hall, Richard H. 1968. "Professionalization and Bureaucratization." *American Sociological Review* 33: 92–104 (Feb.).

Halperin, Morton H. 1974. *Bureaucratic Politics and Foreign Policy*. Washington, D.C.: Brookings Institution.

Hammond, Thomas H. 1986. "Agenda Control, Organizational Structure, and Bureaucratic Politics." *American Journal of Political Science* 30(2): 379–420.

Hayek, F. A. 1945/1984. "The Use of Knowledge in Society." *American Economic Review* 35, No. 4 (Sept. 1945). Reprinted in Chiaki Nishiyama and Kurt Leube, eds. *The Essence of Hayek*. Stanford, Calif.: Hoover Institution Press, 1984.

———. 1978/1984. "Competition as a Discovery Process." In Chiaki Nishiyama and Kurt Leube, eds. *The Essence of Hayek*. Stanford, Calif.: Hoover Institution Press, 1984.

Healy, Paul. 1986. "Interpretive Policy Inquiry: A Response to the Limitations of the Received View." *Policy Sciences* 19: 381–96.

Heclo, Hugh. 1977. *A Government of Strangers*. Washington, D.C.: Brookings Institution.

Hofferbert, Richard I. 1974. *The Study of Public Policy*. New York: Bobbs-Merrill.

Howton, F. William. 1969. *Functionaries*. Chicago: Quadrangle Books.

Hume, David. 1980. *A Treatise on Human Nature*. L. A. Selby-Bigge, ed.; 2d ed. revised by P. H. Nidditch. Oxford: Clarendon.

Jennings, Bruce. 1983. "Interpretive Social Science and Policy Analysis." In Daniel Callahan and Bruce Jennings, eds. *Ethics, the Social Sciences, and Policy Analysis*. New York: Plenum Press.

Kahneman, Daniel, Paul Slovic, and Amos Tversky. 1982. *Judgment Under Uncertainty: Heuristics and Biases*. Cambridge, Eng.: Cambridge University Press.

Kanter, Rosabeth Moss, and Barry A. Stein. 1979. *Life in Organizations: Workplaces as People Experience Them*. New York: Basic Books.

Kaufman, Herbert. 1967. *The Forest Ranger*. Baltimore, Md.: Johns Hopkins Press.

————. 1977. *Red Tape: Its Origins, Uses, and Abuses*. Washington, D.C.: Brookings Institution.

————. 1981. *The Administrative Behavior of Federal Bureau Chiefs*. Washington, D.C.: Brookings Institution.

Kingdon, John W. 1984. *Agendas, Alternatives, and Public Policies*. Boston: Little, Brown.

Kraft, Michael E. 1981. "Congress and the National Energy Policy: Assessing the Policy Making Process." In Regina S. Axelrod, ed. *Environment, Energy, Public Policy: Toward a Rational Future*. Lexington, Mass.: Lexington Books, D. C. Heath.

Kuhn, Thomas S. 1970. *The Structure of Scientific Revolutions*. 2d ed. Chicago: University of Chicago Press.

Lindblom, Charles E. 1959. "The Science of Muddling Through." *Public Administration Review* 19: 79–88.

————. 1965. *The Intelligence of Democracy*. New York: Free Press.

————. 1968. *The Policy-Making Process*. Englewood Cliffs, N.J.: Prentice Hall.

Lindblom, Charles E., and David K. Cohen. 1979. *Usable Knowledge*. New Haven: Yale University Press.

Lipsky, Michael. 1980. *Street Level Bureaucracy: Dilemmas of the Individual in Public Service*. New York: Russell Sage Foundation.

Luce, R. Duncan, and Howard Raiffa. 1957. *Games and Decisions*. New York: Wiley.

Lynn, Laurence E., Jr. 1978. "The Question of Relevance." In L. E. Lynn, ed. *Knowledge and Policy: The Uncertain Connection*. Washington, D.C.: National Academy of Sciences.

MacRae, Duncan. 1981. "Evaluative Problems of Public Policy Analysis." *Research in Public Policy Analysis and Management* 1: 175–94.

March, James G. 1978. "Bounded Rationality, Ambiguity, and the Engineering of Choice." *Bell Journal of Economics* 9: 587–608.

————. 1981. "Decisions in Organization and Theories of Choice." In Andrew Van de Ven and William Joyce, eds. *Assessing Organizational Design and Performance*. New York: Wiley Interscience.

March, James G., and J. P. Olsen, eds. 1976. *Ambiguity and Choice in Organizations*. Bergen: Universitetsforlaget.

March, James G., and G. Sevon. 1984. "Gossip, Information, and Decision Making." In Lee S. Sproull and Patrick D. Larkey, eds. *Advances* in *Information Processing in Organizations*, Vol. 1. Greenwich, Conn.: JAI Press.

March, James G., and Herbert A. Simon. 1958. *Organizations*. New York: Wiley.

Meltsner, Arnold J. 1972. "Political Feasibility and Policy Analysis." *Public Administration Review* Nov./Dec.: 859–67.

———. 1976. *Policy Analysts in the Bureaucracy*. Berkeley, Calif.: University of California Press.

———. 1980. "Creating a Policy Analysis Profession." In Stuart S. Nagel, ed. *Improving Policy Analysis*. Beverly Hills: Sage Publications.

Merton, Robert K. 1936. "The Unanticipated Consequences of Purposive Social Action." *American Sociological Review* 1: 894–904.

Meyer, John W., and Brian Rowan. 1977. "Institutionalized Organization: Formal Structure as Myth and Ceremony." *American Journal of Sociology* 83: 340–63 (Sept.).

Muir, William K., Jr. 1973. *Law and Attitude Change*. Chicago: University of Chicago Press.

Nagel, Stuart S. 1980. "Political Science and Public Administration as Key Elements in Policy Analysis." In Stuart S. Nagel, ed. *Improving Policy Analysis*. Beverly Hills: Sage Publications.

National Energy Transportation Study. 1980. A Preliminary Report to the President by the Secretary of Transportation and the Secretary of Energy, July, 1980.

Nelson, Richard R., and Sidney G. Winter. 1982. *An Evolutionary Theory of Economic Change*. Cambridge, Mass.: Belknap Press.

Nisbett, Richard, and Lee Ross. 1980. *Human Inference: Strategies and Shortcomings of Social Judgment*. Englewood Cliffs, N.J.: Prentice Hall.

Okrent, David. 1981. *Nuclear Reactor Safety: On the History of the Regulatory Process*. Madison: University of Wisconsin Press.

Orlans, Harold. 1973. *Contracting for Knowledge*. San Francisco: Jossey-Bass.

Pfeffer, Jeffrey. 1977. "Power and Resource Allocation in Organizations." In B. M. Staw and G. R. Salancik, eds. *New Directions in Organizational Behavior*. Chicago: St. Clair Press.

Polanyi, Michael. 1962. *Personal Knowledge: Towards a Post-Critical Philosophy*. New York: Harper Torchbooks.

Pressman, Jeffrey L., and Aaron Wildavsky. 1973. *Implementation*. Berkeley, Calif.: University of California Press.

Quade, E. S. 1970. "Why Policy Sciences?" *Policy Sciences* 1(1): 1–2.

Rein, Martin. 1976. *Social Science and Public Policy*. New York: Penguin Books.

Rich, Robert F. 1981a. "Knowledge in Society." In R. F. Rich, ed. *The Knowledge Cycle.* Beverly Hills: Sage Publications.

————. 1981b. *Social Science Information and Public Policy Making.* San Francisco: Jossey-Bass.

————. 1982. "The Production of Useful Knowledge: Revisiting Traditional Organizational and Bureaucratic Theory." Prepared for a research conference on "Producing Useful Knowledge for Organizations" at the University of Pittsburgh, Oct. 28–30, 1982.

Riker, William H. 1986. *The Art of Political Manipulation.* New Haven, Conn.: Yale University Press.

Rittel, Horst W. J., and Melvin M. Webber. 1973. "Dilemmas in a General Theory of Planning." *Policy Sciences* 4: 155–69.

Rosenbaum, Walter A. 1981. "Notes from No-Man's Land: The Politics and Ecology of Energy Research and Development." In Regina S. Axelrod, ed. *Environment, Energy, Public Policy: Toward a Rational Future.* Lexington, Mass.: Lexington Books, D. C. Heath.

Rudwick, Martin J. S. 1985. *The Meaning of Fossils: Episodes in the History of Paleontology.* Chicago: University of Chicago Press.

Rule, James B. 1978. *Insight and Social Betterment.* New York: Oxford University Press.

Schneider, Janet A., Nancy J. Stevens, and Louis G. Tornatzky. 1982. "Policy Research and Analysis: An Empirical Profile, 1975–80." *Policy Sciences* 15: 99–114.

Schott, Richard L. 1976. "Public Administration as a Profession: Problems and Prospects." *Public Administration Review* 36: 253–59.

Schutz, Alfred. 1967. *The Phenomenology of the Social World.* Evanston, Ill.: Northwestern University Press.

————. 1970. *Reflections on the Problem of Relevance.* New Haven: Yale University Press.

Schutz, Alfred, and Thomas Luckmann. 1973. *The Structures of the Life-World.* Evanston, Ill.: Northwestern University Press.

Scott, W. Richard. 1981. *Organizations: Rational, Natural and Open Systems.* Englewood Cliffs, N.J.: Prentice Hall.

Selznick, Philip. 1949. *TVA and the Grass Roots.* Berkeley, Calif.: University of California Press.

Simon, Herbert A. 1956. "Rational Choices and the Structure of the Environment." *Psychological Review* 63: 129–38.

————. 1978. "Rationality as Process and as Product of Thought," from the Richard T. Ely lecture. *American Economic Review* 68: 1–16.

————. 1981. *The Sciences of the Artificial.* Cambridge, Mass.: MIT Press.

Simon, Herbert A., Donald W. Smithburg, and Victor A. Thompson. 1950. *Public Administration.* New York: Knopf.

Skolnick, Jerome H. 1975. *Justice Without Trial: Law Enforcement in Democratic Society.* New York: Wiley.

Smith, Richard A. 1984. "Advocacy, Interpretation and Influence in the U.S. Congress." *American Political Science Review* 78: 44–63 (Mar.).

Sproull, Lee S., Stephen S. Weiner, and David Wolf. 1977. *Organizing an Anarchy.* Chicago: University of Chicago Press.

Steinbruner, John D. 1974. *The Cybernetic Theory of Decision: New Dimensions of Political Analysis.* Princeton, N.J.: Princeton University Press.

Stever, Donald W., Jr. 1980. *Seabrook and the Nuclear Regulatory Commission: The Licensing of a Nuclear Power Plant.* Hanover, N.H.: University of New England Press.

Stinchcombe, Arthur L. 1974. *Creating Efficient Industrial Administrations.* New York: Academic Press.

Sugden, Robert, and Alan Williams. 1978. *The Principles of Practical Cost-Benefit Analysis.* Oxford: Oxford University Press.

Sutton, Robert I. 1984. *Organization Death.* Ph.D. diss., University of Michigan.

Taylor, F. W. 1911. *Scientific Management.* New York: Harper & Row.

Taylor, Michael. 1975. "The Theory of Collective Choice." In F. I. Greenstein and N. W. Polsby, eds. *Handbook of Political Science,* Vol. 3. Reading, Mass.: Addison-Wesley.

Taylor, Serge. 1984. *Making Bureaucracies Think.* Stanford, Calif.: Stanford University Press.

Thompson, James D. 1967. *Organizations in Action.* New York: McGraw-Hill.

Torgerson, Douglas. 1986a. "Between Knowledge and Politics: Three Faces of Policy Analysis." *Policy Sciences* 19: 33–59.

———. 1986b. "Interpretive Policy Inquiry: A Response to Its Limitations." *Policy Sciences* 19: 397–405.

Watson, James D. 1968. *The Double Helix: A Personal Account of the Discovery of the Structure of DNA.* New York: Atheneum.

Weatherley, Richard, and Michael Lipsky. 1977. "Street-Level Bureaucrats and Institutional Innovation: Implementing Special Education Reform." *Harvard Education Review* 47(2): 171–97.

Weber, Max. 1946. "Bureaucracy." In H. H. Gerth and C. Wright Mills, eds. *From Max Weber.* New York: Oxford University Press.

———. 1978. *Economy and Society.* Guenther Roth and Claus Wittich, eds. Berkeley, Calif.: University of California Press.

Weick, Karl E. 1979. *The Social Psychology of Organizing.* New York: Random House.

Weimer, David L., and Aidan R. Vining. 1988. *Policy Analysis: Concepts and Practice.* Englewood Cliffs, N.J.: Prentice Hall.

Weiner, Stephen S. 1976. "Participation, Deadlines, and Choice." In J. G. March and J. P. Olsen, eds. *Ambiguity and Choice in Organizations.* Bergen: Universitetsforlaget.

Weiss, Carol H. 1977. "Research for Policy's Sake: The Enlightenment Function of Social Science Research." *Policy Analysis* 3: 531–45.

———. 1978. "Improving the Linkage Between Social Research and Public Policy." In L. E. Lynn, ed. *Knowledge and Policy: The Uncertain Connection.* Washington, D.C.: National Academy of Sciences.

———. 1980. "Knowledge Creep and Decision Accretion." *Knowledge: Creation, Diffusion, Utilization.* 1: 381–404.

Weiss, Carol H., and Michael J. Bucuvalas. 1980. *Social Science Research and Decision-Making.* New York: Columbia University Press.

Weiss, Janet A., and Judith E. Gruber. 1984. "Using Knowledge for Control in Fragmented Policy Arenas." *Journal of Policy Analysis and Management* 3: 225–47.

Wildavsky, Aaron. 1979. *Speaking Truth to Power: The Art and Craft of Policy Analysis.* Boston: Little, Brown.

———. 1984. *The Politics of the Budgetary Process,* 4th ed. Boston: Little, Brown.

Wildavsky, Aaron, and Ellen Tenenbaum. 1981. *The Politics of Mistrust: Estimating American Oil and Gas Resources.* Beverly Hills: Sage Publications.

Wilensky, Harold L. 1964. "The Professionalization of Everyone?" *American Journal of Sociology* 70: 137–58.

———. 1967. *Organizational Intelligence.* New York: Basic Books.

Williamson, Oliver E. 1975. *Markets and Hierarchies: Analysis and Antitrust Implications.* New York: Free Press.

———. 1981. "The Economics of Organization: The Transaction Cost Approach." Working Paper no. 96. Philadelphia: Center for the Study of Organizational Innovation, University of Pennsylvania.

Wohlstetter, Roberta. 1962. *Pearl Harbor.* Stanford, Calif.: Stanford University Press.

Index

Library of Congress Cataloging-in-Publication Data

Feldman, Martha S.,
    Order without design: information production and
policy making / Martha S. Feldman.
      p.   cm.
    Bibliography: p.
    Includes index.
    ISBN 0-8047-1724-9 (alk. paper). ISBN 0-8047-1726-5 (pbk.)
    1. Government report writing.   2. Political
planning. I. Title.
JF1525.R46F45 1989
350'.0006—dc19   88-34255
                                            CIP